TOEIC® L&R Test 実践チャレンジ

 編著

西谷 恒志
Tom Dillon
Michael Schauerte

TSURUMI SHOTEN

スコア 550〜600 をめざす
TOEIC® L&R Test 実践チャレンジ

Copyright © 2025 by
NISHIYA Koji, Tom Dillon, Michael Schauerte
and TSURUMI SHOTEN

All rights reserved

画像 (p. 130)：
©Amerigo_images–Fotolia.com

自習用音声について

本書の自習用音声は以下よりダウンロードできます。予習，復習にご利用ください。
（2025 年 4 月 1 日開始予定）

http://www.otowatsurumi.com/00615/

URL はブラウザのアドレスバーに直接入力して下さい。

音声の記号とトラック番号について

 〜 　自習用音声のトラック番号です。

 〜 　Review Test のトラック番号です。（教授用）

はじめに

　TOEIC® テストは、1979 年に第一回テストが実施されて以来、長い歴史があります。このテストが始まった 1970 年代、多くの日本企業は海外に進出していきました。海外における企業活動は、当然、人と人、国と国の相互理解の基に行われます。多くの日本人が英語によるコミュニケーション能力を磨く必要性が急速に増大したのです。こうした時代を背景に、国際ビジネスの最前線で求められる「実際のコミュニケーションに必要な能力を客観的に評価し、併せてその評価を目標設定にできる世界共通のモノサシ」（一般財団法人 国際ビジネスコミュニケーション協会、https://www.iibc-global.org/toeic/toeic_program/philosophy.html）として、TOEIC L&R が開発されたのです。

　わずか約 3,000 人の受験者で始まった TOEIC® テストは、毎年受験者数を伸ばし、1990 年度には 332,000 人、2000 年度には 100 万人を突破し、2023 年度には個人・企業・団体・学校合わせて、年間約 192 万人に達しています。

　では、大学生にとって身近な就職と TOEIC® テストの関係について見ていきましょう。国際ビジネスコミュニケーション協会による最新のデータ「英語活用実態調査 2022（企業・団体）によると、企業・団体が今後のビジネスパーソンに求める知識・スキルとしては、「英語」が 74.5% と最も高くなっています。これと同じ意味で、社員・職員に不足している、今後強化する必要がある知識・スキルについても、「英語」が第 1 位で 55.0% となっています。

　このような企業・団体側のニーズもあり、TOEIC® テストのスコアを新卒採用時に「要件としている」「参考としている」「要件・参考とする可能性がある」と回答した企業の割合は合わせて 73.6% にも上っています。ただ、350 点や 400 点のスコアは武器になりません。エントリーシートでアピールできる（＝企業・団体側が新入社員に求める）スコアは、平均で 550 点なのです。

　本書は、この 550 点から 600 点を目指すべく、これまで数多く出されている公式ガイドブックの分析を基に、さらに最新の公式ガイドブックを分析して、パート別に頻出の傾向に沿った実践問題をまとめてあります。

　TOEIC® テストのスコアは基本的に学習時間と比例します。傾向に沿った数多くの実践問題を解くトレーニングを行うことが唯一無二の方法です。本書の実践問題で行うトレーニングを継続していくことでスコアアップが実現する、本書がその一助となれば幸いです。

2024 年 11 月

編著者代表
西 谷 恒 志

【ユニットの内容について】

　各ユニットはリーディングとリスニングの各セクションからの実践問題を組み合わせて、1 ユニットあたりの量とバランスに配慮をしています。各ユニットとも、実践問題で扱われる単語・熟語のうち、特に重要と思われるものをターゲットとした Warm-up 問題を冒頭に配し、実践問題チャレンジにスムーズに進めるように構成しています。

【レビューテストについて】

　巻末に 2 回分収録した Review Test は、PART 1 から PART 7 を網羅したもので、1 回のテストは、「リスニングセクション 50 問 + リーディングセクション 50 問の計 100 問」で実際の TOEIC® テストの半分の量となっています。

　Review Test 1 は、Unit 1 ～ Unit 6 で学習した各 Part の出題形式に、Review Test 2 は、全 Unit で学習した各 Part の出題形式に準じています。Review Test 1 は期中の中間テスト的に使用したり、Uni 6 までの復習テストとして使用したりすることができます。Review Test 2 は、全 Unit の復習テストとして使用したり、科目の修了テストとして使用したりすることができます。

　本書は、『TOEIC® Test LISTENING SECTION 実践演習』『TOEIC® Test READING SECTION 実践演習』（共に音羽書房鶴見書店、2017 年刊）からの問題を厳選して一部再収録し、これに近年の出題傾向をふまえた新規問題を数多く追加して再編集したものです。

Table of Contents

Unit 1: 写真描写問題／会話問題／短文穴埋め問題／長文穴埋め問題 ···· 1

Unit 2: 写真描写問題／会話問題／短文穴埋め問題／長文穴埋め問題 ···· 8

Unit 3: 応答問題／会話問題／説明文問題／読解問題 ················ 14

Unit 4: 会話問題／説明文問題／短文穴埋め問題／長文穴埋め問題 ····· 20

Unit 5: 応答問題／説明文問題／短文穴埋め問題／読解問題 ·········· 26

Unit 6: 応答問題／説明文問題／短文穴埋め問題／読解問題 ·········· 31

Unit 7: 写真描写問題／会話問題／短文穴埋め問題／長文穴埋め問題 ··· 37

Unit 8: 応答問題／会話問題／説明文問題／読解問題 ················ 44

Unit 9: 応答問題／会話問題／説明文問題／読解問題 ················ 50

Unit 10: 応答問題／会話問題／説明文問題／読解問題 ················ 56

Unit 11: 説明文問題／読解問題 ································· 62

Unit 12: 説明文問題／読解問題 ································· 68

Unit 13: 説明文問題／読解問題 ································· 75

Review Test 1 ··· 81

Review Test 2 ··· 105

解答用紙 ·· 133

v

Listening Section				Reading Section		
Part 1	Part 2	Part 3	Part 4	Part 5	Part 6	Part 7

Unit 1 写真描写問題／会話問題／短文穴埋め問題／長文穴埋め問題

Warm-Up ///

次の 1. ～ 7. の英文について、------- に入れるべき最も適当なものを (A), (B) より選びなさい。
（カッコ内はこの Unit 中の関連パートを表します。〈例〉Pt3 = Part 3)

1. This train is an express, you'll have to catch a ------- at platform 3. (Pt3)
   (A) native   (B) local

2. Mark has ------- places he wants to visit this summer, and it's hard to choose
   just one. (Pt3)
   (A) a piece of   (B) a bunch of

3. Clayton usually ------- traveling during rush hour to escape heavy traffic. (Pt3)
   (A) avoids   (B) pursues

4. Our marketing strategy should be ------- our company's mission and values.
   (Pt6)
   (A) in line with   (B) by way of

5. The idea was ------- and sparked a lot of interest among the investors. (Pt6)
   (A) original   (B) common

6. It is safer to cross the road at a ------- crossing. (Pt1)
   (A) railroad   (B) pedestrian

7. "What a ------- !" Mom cried as she saw the dirty room. (Pt3)
   (A) deal   (B) mess

1

1. [PART 1] 写真描写問題

Points

- 「一人」が写っている写真を取り扱う。"人の動作・状態"を中心に聞き取ろう。
- 人の動作を示す動詞としては、carry, cook, cut, drive, gather, hold, plant, read, remove, ride, stand, sweep, wash などの基本的な動詞のほか、bend down, shovel off, take a bite などの熟語も散見される。
- 状態を表す動詞は、モノが主語のセンテンスにおいて、be loaded, be sliced, be taken down のように受動態で用いられることが多い。

次の 1.～2. の写真について、それぞれの写真を説明する英文が 4 つ聞こえてきます。最も適切な英文を (A)～(D) より選び、その記号をマークしなさい。

 No.1

Ⓐ　Ⓑ　Ⓒ　Ⓓ

 No. 2

Ⓐ　Ⓑ　Ⓒ　Ⓓ

2. [PART 3] 会話問題

> **Points**
>
> 音変化を中心にピックアップ
> * M-1 は男性の1番目の発話、W-2 は女性の2番目の発話を表します。
> Questions 1 through 3 の会話： (M-1) It goes all the way to (W-2) need to get off then (M-2) have to catch a local (M-3) won't have to wait
> Questions 4 through 6 の会話： (M-1) It's a mess! (W-1) for a long time (M-2) leaving them in there (W-2) mention it to Ms. Johnson

2つの会話を聞き、それぞれの会話に関する3つの質問文の答えとして最も適切なものを (A) ～ (D) より選び、その記号をマークしなさい。

1. What mistake has the woman made?
   (A) She's has taken the express train.
   (B) She has taken the local train.
   (C) She has stopped at Grace Avenue.
   (D) She has gone to Woodville.

2. What does the woman need to do?
   (A) She needs to change trains at Grace Avenue.
   (B) She needs to change trains at Woodville.
   (C) She needs to find the next station.
   (D) She needs to take a different express.

3. What does the man advise that she do?
   (A) He suggests she get off at Grace Avenue.
   (B) He can't say what to do.
   (C) He tells her to catch an express from Woodville.
   (D) He tells her to catch a local from Woodville.

04. 4. What problem does the refrigerator have?
    (A) There are a couple of PET bottles.
    (B) There are not enough bottles.
    (C) It is half-empty.
    (D) It is full.

    Ⓐ Ⓑ Ⓒ Ⓓ

5. What does Beth think about the refrigerator?
    (A) It should be used more often.
    (B) There are no problems.
    (C) Fewer people should use it.
    (D) Something needs to be done.

    Ⓐ Ⓑ Ⓒ Ⓓ

6. What is going to happen next Friday?
    (A) Beth and Todd are going to mention the problem.
    (B) Ms. Johnson is going to solve the problem.
    (C) A staff meeting will be held outside the meeting room.
    (D) Beth and Todd will write their names on the bottles.

    Ⓐ Ⓑ Ⓒ Ⓓ

Unit 1: 写真描写問題／会話問題／短文穴埋め問題／長文穴埋め問題

3. [PART 5] 短文穴埋め問題

Points

1. 雇うのか、雇われるのか。2. 地位に満足しないときは。3. entering a foreign airport とある。
4. for the moviegoers がキー。5. クルマの新しいモデルがどうなった？

次の 1.~5. の英文について、------- に入れるべき最も適切なものをそれぞれ (A) ～ (D) の中から選び、その記号をマークしなさい。

1. The new ------- who joined the sales department has excellent customer service skills.
   (A) employment   (B) employed
   (C) employee   (D) employer   Ⓐ Ⓑ Ⓒ Ⓓ

2. Mr. Jones was unhappy with his posting in a foreign country, so he asked for a -------.
   (A) career   (B) transfer
   (C) shift   (D) promotion   Ⓐ Ⓑ Ⓒ Ⓓ

3. Upon entering a foreign airport, passengers are required to pass through ------- and customs. (RU)
   (A) emigration   (B) immigration
   (C) migration   (D) border   Ⓐ Ⓑ Ⓒ Ⓓ

4. The price of ------- was too much for the moviegoers.
   (A) admit   (B) admission
   (C) admitting   (D) admittance
                                                  Ⓐ Ⓑ Ⓒ Ⓓ

5. The ------- of SmartClean Auto's new model has been delayed by three months due to a parts shortage.
   (A) launch   (B) terminal
   (C) exploration   (D) construction
                                                  Ⓐ Ⓑ Ⓒ Ⓓ

5

4. [PART 6] 長文穴埋め問題

Points

依頼主からデザイナーへ宛てたメール。主題は広告ポスターのサンプル。
1. ポスターは制作済かどうか。 2. 空欄の直前の them が指すものは？ 3. "centering information" と "put it on the right side" との関係は？ 4. 空欄と前文との関係、ポスターに対する Mark の評価は？

次の英文中の 1.~4. の空所に入れるべき最も適切なものをそれぞれ (A)~(D) の中から選び、その記号をマークしなさい。

To: Jennifer Hanson <jhanson@bestart.com>

From: Mark Anderson <manderson@createevent.com>

Date: 3 March

Subject: Poster

Dear Ms. Hanson,

Thank you for sending the sample of the advertisement poster. I've shown it to my staff and they are very satisfied with the work --------. We would like to suggest a few changes to the colors and the text but mostly it's in line with what we were thinking. There's a little too much space surrounding the man and woman. Could you please make them --------? Also, what do you think of changing the color of the main title from light blue to a darker blue? -------- centering information such as the date, place, and time of the event, please put it on the right side of the poster just below the photo of the man and woman. By the way, the symbol you designed for the event, is original and interesting. -------- Thank you for your hard work.

Sincerely,

Mark Anderson

---

1. (A) you were going to do   (B) you'll do
   (C) you've done   (D) you'll be doing

           Ⓐ   Ⓑ   Ⓒ   Ⓓ

6

Unit 1: 写真描写問題／会話問題／短文穴埋め問題／長文穴埋め問題

2. (A) more colorful   (B) smaller
   (C) less colorful   (D) bigger

Ⓐ Ⓑ Ⓒ Ⓓ

3. (A) Instead of   (B) Because of
   (C) As if   (D) Even though

Ⓐ Ⓑ Ⓒ Ⓓ

4. (A) But we will adopt your poster design.
   (B) Therefore we would like you to change it.
   (C) We think with these few changes the poster will be perfect.
   (D) We always feel it pleasant to make a poster redesign.

Ⓐ Ⓑ Ⓒ Ⓓ

Listening Section				Reading Section		
Part 1	Part 2	Part 3	Part 4	Part 5	Part 6	Part 7

Unit 2 写真描写問題／会話問題／短文穴埋め問題／長文穴埋め問題

次の 1.〜7. の英文について、------- に入れるべき最も適当なものを (A), (B) より選びなさい。
（カッコ内はこの Unit 中の関連パートを表します。〈例〉Pt3 = Part 3）

1. Our department is going to split into two ------- next month. (Pt3)
   (A) divisions   (B) partitions

2. Gavin is ------- the new project and manages the schedules for the whole team. (Pt3)
   (A) at the top of   (B) in charge of

3. Reducing ------- is not the only way to increase a company's profits. (Pt3)
   (A) costs   (B) revenues

4. When you buy this new phone, you have ------- different colors. (Pt3)
   (A) an advantage over   (B) a choice of

5. To ensure quality control, we regularly ------- the production process. (Pt6)
   (A) require   (B) verify

6. Robert suffered a bad ------- in the car accident but survived. (Pt6)
   (A) infection   (B) injury

7. During the disaster relief efforts, volunteers were ------- to help distribute food and supplies. (Pt6)
   (A) assigning   (B) assigned

8

Unit 2: 写真描写問題／会話問題／短文穴埋め問題／長文穴埋め問題

1. [PART 1] 写真描写問題

Points
- 2つの写真には「複数の人」が写っているので、"それぞれの人の動作・状態"を中心に聞き取ろう。
- また、「手や足の状態」や「身に着けているモノ」についても注意を払うことが大切。
- 通常は、遠くに小さく見えるものや写真の片隅にある小物に関する描写はされない。

次の1.〜2.の写真について、それぞれの写真を説明する英文が4つ聞こえてきます。最も適切な英文を(A)〜(D)より選び、その記号をマークしなさい。

🎧05 **No.1**

Ⓐ Ⓑ Ⓒ Ⓓ

🎧06 **No. 2**

Ⓐ Ⓑ Ⓒ Ⓓ

9

2. [PART 3] 会話問題

> **Points**
>
> 音変化を中心にピックアップ
> * M-1 は男性の1番目、W-2 は、女性の2番目の発話を表します。
> Questions 1 through 3 の会話: (M-1) some of them are perfect (W-1) I could meet you (M-2) I will be out of town; on a business trip (W-2) let's meet on Thursday
> Questions 4 through 6 の会話: (M-1) The cost of the pens is $700 (W-1) what color will the name and phone number be? (M-2) a choice of black or blue ink in the pens (W-2) We definitely want black ink.

4つの会話を聞き、それぞれの会話に関する3つの質問文の答えとして最も適切なものを (A)〜(D) より選び、その記号をマークしなさい。

1. What is the man interested in discussing?
   (A) Management
   (B) Services
   (C) His division
   (D) Purchasing

   Ⓐ Ⓑ Ⓒ Ⓓ

2. What did the woman tell the man?
   (A) She handles the purchasing.
   (B) She will be on a business trip.
   (C) She will discuss her services.
   (D) She is always at work on Mondays.

   Ⓐ Ⓑ Ⓒ Ⓓ

3. What did the man and woman decide?
   (A) To take a business trip next week
   (B) To meet in either Chicago or Detroit
   (C) To discuss business in her office
   (D) To exchange company catalogs

   Ⓐ Ⓑ Ⓒ Ⓓ

4. What are they mainly talking about?
   (A) A report
   (B) A sign
   (C) An order
   (D) A telephone

   Ⓐ Ⓑ Ⓒ Ⓓ

5. What does the woman ask the man about?
   (A) The color of the cover
   (B) The color of the printing
   (C) The color of the envelope
   (D) The color of the paper

   Ⓐ Ⓑ Ⓒ Ⓓ

6. What color ink does the woman choose?
   (A) Red
   (B) Black
   (C) Blue
   (D) Green

   Ⓐ Ⓑ Ⓒ Ⓓ

3. [PART 5] 短文穴埋め問題

Points

1. 売り上げが悪いので…。2.「動詞 + 目的語 +to 不定詞」の構文をとるものは？ 3. from his account とあるので…。4. 検証するのか、検証されるのか？　5.「別の道を見つけた」

次の 1.〜5. の英文について、------- に入れるべき最も適切なものをそれぞれ (A)〜(D) の中から選び、その記号をマークしなさい。

1. The employer had to ------- two employees because of the continuing short sales.
   - (A) discriminate
   - (B) disorder
   - (C) disintegrate
   - (D) dismiss

   Ⓐ Ⓑ Ⓒ Ⓓ

2. The city council ------- everyone to participate in the community clean-up event.
   - (A) reports
   - (B) considers
   - (C) encourages
   - (D) recognizes

   Ⓐ Ⓑ Ⓒ Ⓓ

3. Anyone who ------- funds from his account is just asking for trouble.
   - (A) overdraws
   - (B) overcharges
   - (C) overflows
   - (D) overbids

   Ⓐ Ⓑ Ⓒ Ⓓ

4. The accuracy of the sales report was ------- by an independent auditor.
   - (A) verifies
   - (B) verified
   - (C) verifying
   - (D) verification

   Ⓐ Ⓑ Ⓒ Ⓓ

5. Main Street was ------- with traffic but I was able to find another road.
   - (A) mixed
   - (B) charged
   - (C) jammed
   - (D) bound

   Ⓐ Ⓑ Ⓒ Ⓓ

12

4. [PART 6] 長文穴埋め問題

Points

ミルウォーキーを襲った竜巻に関するニュース記事。1. 空欄の前に still があるので。2. 電力会社の広報担当者がすることは？ 3. 電力会社が電力の回復時期を伝える最も自然な言い方。4. 竜巻が襲った地域は？

次の英文中の 1.~4. の空所に入れるべき最も適切なものをそれぞれ (A)~(D) の中から選び、その記号をマークしなさい。

Milwaukee (July 11) — The community of Grover Heights is still ------- electric
1.
power today after a Category 1 tornado struck the town on Monday evening.
The storm uprooted trees and caused extensive damage to rooftops, as well
as severing powerlines. No injuries have been -------, but Central Electric
2.
Company spokesperson Edith Wentz has stated it may take ------- for power
3.
to be restored. In the interim, a relief unit from the local National Guard has
been assigned to help any Grover Heights residents with emergency needs. The
tornado was part of a ------- range of storms that caused havoc all across Cole
4.
and Mason counties on Monday.

---

1. (A) using   (B) with   (C) without   (D) against

                                                          Ⓐ   Ⓑ   Ⓒ   Ⓓ

2. (A) denied   (B) reported   (C) allowed   (D) observed

                                                             Ⓐ   Ⓑ   Ⓒ   Ⓓ

3. (A) until Thursday morning or later
   (B) until Thursday morning or earlier
   (C) after Thursday morning or afternoon
   (D) after Thursday or Friday

                                                             Ⓐ   Ⓑ   Ⓒ   Ⓓ

4. (A) narrow   (B) deep   (C) exact   (D) wide

                                                           Ⓐ   Ⓑ   Ⓒ   Ⓓ

Listening Section				Reading Section		
Part 1	Part 2	Part 3	Part 4	Part 5	Part 6	Part 7

Unit 3 応答問題／会話問題／説明文問題／読解問題

Warm-Up

次の 1. ～ 7. の英文について、------- に入れるべき最も適当なものを (A), (B) より選びなさい。
（カッコ内はこの Unit 中の関連パートを表します。〈例〉Pt3 = Part 3）

1. Just because you continue training doesn't mean you'll see results -------.
   (Pt2)
   (A) in no time　　　　　　　　　(B) behind time

2. Professor Richard Thompson has been asked to ------- the panel discussion on marketing. (Pt2)
   (A) chair　　　　　　　　　(B) table

3. TechTech's annual revenue reached impressive -------, surpassing $10 million last year. (Pt3)
   (A) figures　　　　　　　　　(B) numerals

4. Our annual ------- increased from $1.7 million to $5.4 million last year. (Pt3)
   (A) earnings　　　　　　　　　(B) earning

5. Business-class passengers enjoy the ------- of accessing exclusive airport lounges. (Pt4)
   (A) primary　　　　　　　　　(B) privilege

6. The spa offers a ------- massage for first-time visitors. (Pt4)
   (A) complimentary　　　　　　　　　(B) priceless

7. The shareholders' meeting really ------- better than expected. (Pt7)
   (A) turned in　　　　　　　　　(B) turned out

14

Unit 3: 応答問題／会話問題／説明文問題／読解問題

1. [PART 2] 応答問題

Points

① 今回は質問文が「提案」「依頼・許可」「判断・評価」を表す問題を扱う。
② 「提案」に関する質問文としては、Why don't you[we] ...?, Why not ...?, Would you like to ...?, Would you like ＋人＋ to ...? などがある。
③ 「依頼・許可」に関する表現としては、Please ...?, Will[Would] you (please) ...?, Won't you ...?, Can[Could] you ...? などがよく使われる。
④ 「判断・評価」に関する表現としては、付加疑問文や Are you sure ...? の他に、「重要かどうか」「良し悪し」など、いろいろな問いかけがある。

英文が聞こえ、その英文につづいて (A)(B)(C) 3 つの応答文が聞こえます。1.~5. の英文に対する最も適切な応答文を (A)~(C) の中から選び、その記号をマークしなさい。

09 1. Mark your answer on your sheet.

(A)　(B)　(C)

2. Mark your answer on your sheet.

(A)　(B)　(C)

3. Mark your answer on your sheet.

(A)　(B)　(C)

4. Mark your answer on your sheet.

(A)　(B)　(C)

5. Mark your answer on your sheet.

(A)　(B)　(C)

2. [PART 3] 会話問題

> **Points**
> Questions 1 through 3: 話題は、会社の売上高。2. は表現の意図を問う質問。音変化としては、looking at them; get it; year on year; figure out a way

会話を聞き、それぞれの会話に関する3つの質問文の答えとして最も適切なものを (A)〜(D) より選び、その記号をマークしなさい。

1. What did the man say he was doing?
    (A) Looking at the sales figures
    (B) Trying to increase sales
    (C) Studying the overhead costs
    (D) Streamlining operations

    Ⓐ Ⓑ Ⓒ Ⓓ

2. What does the man imply when he says, "starting with our overseas branches"?
    (A) He's looking forward to seeing the manager.
    (B) He wants to recheck the sales figures.
    (C) He needs to visit the overseas branches.
    (D) He thinks overseas operations are inefficient.

    Ⓐ Ⓑ Ⓒ Ⓓ

3. What does the man think the company should do?
    (A) Open new overseas branches
    (B) Introduce more operations
    (C) Improve its efficiency
    (D) Figure out how to boost sales

    Ⓐ Ⓑ Ⓒ Ⓓ

Unit 3: 応答問題／会話問題／説明文問題／読解問題

3. [PART 4] 説明文問題

Points

質問文の先読みから、聞き取りのポイントをピックアップ
Questions 1 through 3: 何についての広告なのか？　特典を得られる条件・地域、無料の駐車場
がある場所は？

1つの説明文が聞こえてきます。その説明文に関する 1.～3. の質問文の答えとして最も適切な
ものを (A)～(D) より選び、その記号をマークしなさい。

1. What is this advertisement about?
   (A) Online shopping
   (B) Credit card
   (C) Travel agency
   (D) Tourism club

   Ⓐ　Ⓑ　Ⓒ　Ⓓ

2. What is one of the privileges of being a Passport Gold Club member?
   (A) One free night per year
   (B) Luxury cruises at low prices
   (C) Priority reservations at many great restaurants
   (D) VIP lounge access

   Ⓐ　Ⓑ　Ⓒ　Ⓓ

3. Where is parking free?
   (A) At 140 restaurants
   (B) At 140 golf courses
   (C) At 140 hotels
   (D) At 140 car rentals

   Ⓐ　Ⓑ　Ⓒ　Ⓓ

17

4. ［PART 7］読解問題

Points

1つの文書
設問 1–2: ユーザーとサポートとのやりとり。トピックは、ログインできないトラブル。1. サポートは同じ人？ 2. Ed の気持ちは？

次の Text-message chain を読んで、1.～2. の答えとして最も適切なものを、それぞれ (A)～(D) の中から選び、その記号をマークしなさい。

Ed   **Monday 15:15**
I keep getting an error message when I try to login. My user name and password are correct. What's up?

Matt   **Tuesday 18:10**
Hi, this is Matt at Tech Support. We looked into your login situation and find no problems on this end. Still having troubles?

Ed   **Tuesday 19:55**
I don't have any problems here at home, but can't login at my office. I've tried a million times!

Susan   **Thursday 10:30**
Hi, this is Susan at Tech Support. We suggest you speak to your system engineer at work. Something there might be messing things up.

Ed   **Thursday 11:15**
They say we've had no changes whatsoever. I still can't login.

Ed   **Thursday 11:50**
Hey, I've got it! Turns out I had a keyboard problem. One key was sticking, the "plus" sign. I hardly use it except in my password. I'm OK now.

Rich   **Friday 16:45**
Hi this is Rich at Tech Support. Glad to know all is well. Let us know if we can be of further service.

18

1. What can be assumed about the Tech Support staff?
   (A) They have no interest in Ed's problem.
   (B) They rotate in handling Ed's messages.
   (C) They respond promptly to user inquiries.
   (D) They have never encountered such a problem.

   Ⓐ Ⓑ Ⓒ Ⓓ

2. On Tuesday at 7:55 P.M., what does Ed imply when he writes, "I've tried a million times!"?
   (A) He has been counting his login attempts.
   (B) He doesn't believe Tech Support is trying to help him.
   (C) He wishes to impress Tech Support with his efforts.
   (D) He wants to express his frustration.

   Ⓐ Ⓑ Ⓒ Ⓓ

Listening Section				Reading Section		
Part 1	Part 2	Part 3	Part 4	Part 5	Part 6	Part 7

Unit 4 会話問題／説明文問題／短文穴埋め問題／長文穴埋め問題

Warm-Up

次の 1. ～ 7. の英文について、------- に入れるべき最も適当なものを (A), (B) より選びなさい。
（カッコ内はこの Unit 中の関連パートを表します。〈例〉Pt3 = Part 3）

1. Sophia's house is ------- to the park, making it easy to take an early morning walk. (Pt3)
   (A) close   (B) closed

2. Wearing jeans to a client meeting was considered too ------- by my boss. (Pt3)
   (A) attentive   (B) casual

3. Are you more ------- with the room temperature now? (Pt3)
   (A) comfortably   (B) comfortable

4. We invited everyone to the party, including our neighbors and colleagues, ------- those who are out of town. (Pt4)
   (A) despite   (B) except

5. Evelin's ------- to the hospital was quick because of the severity of her condition. (Pt4)
   (A) admission   (B) application

6. Randy ------- his skills with the job requirements before applying. (Pt6)
   (A) matched   (B) blended

7. Matthew is ------- his childhood friends and often remembers their childhood adventures. (Pt6)
   (A) delightful of   (B) fond of

20

Unit 4: 会話問題／説明文問題／短文穴埋め問題／長文穴埋め問題

1. [PART 3] 会話問題

Points

音変化を中心にピックアップ
＊M-1 は男性の1番目、W-2 は、女性の2番目の発話を表します。
Questions 1 through 3 の会話：(W-1) look great (M-1) joined a new gym (W-2) is close to home (M-2) Mine is on 2nd Avenue
Questions 4 through 6 の会話：(W-1) it's a good idea (M-1) it's cool and today ...; is going to get up to 30 degrees (W-2) put on a different tie (M-2) I'll just run down to

2つの会話を聞き、それぞれの会話に関する3つの質問文の答えとして最も適切なものを (A) 〜 (D) より選び、その記号をマークしなさい。

1. Where does this conversation take place?
    (A) At the gym
    (B) On 2nd Avenue
    (C) In their office
    (D) At her home

    Ⓐ Ⓑ Ⓒ Ⓓ

2. Why does the woman want to know the name of the gym?
    (A) She wants to be much better.
    (B) She wants to take more vitamins.
    (C) She wants to change to a gym near her home.
    (D) She wants to change to a gym with a pool.

    Ⓐ Ⓑ Ⓒ Ⓓ

3. What is near the woman's gym?
    (A) Their office
    (B) His doctor
    (C) The city pool
    (D) The woman's home

    Ⓐ Ⓑ Ⓒ Ⓓ

21

13 4. What is the woman concerned about the man?

    (A) His suit is made of wool.

    (B) His suit is too expensive.

    (C) His suit is old-fashioned.

    (D) His suit is not appropriate.

Ⓐ   Ⓑ   Ⓒ   Ⓓ

5. Who most likely is the man?

    (A) A clothing designer

    (B) Her coworker

    (C) A department store clerk

    (D) A salesperson

Ⓐ   Ⓑ   Ⓒ   Ⓓ

6. Why didn't the man wear a dark suit?

    (A) It was too hot.

    (B) It was too casual.

    (C) It didn't match the tie.

    (D) The color was too dark.

Ⓐ   Ⓑ   Ⓒ   Ⓓ

Unit 4: 会話問題／説明文問題／短文穴埋め問題／長文穴埋め問題

2. [PART 4] 説明文問題

Points

質問文の先読みから、聞き取りのポイントをピックアップ
Questions 1 through 3: 大人の入場料は？ 高齢者の割引は？ including 以下と except 以下を聞き取ること。このメッセージが流れるのはいつか？

1つの説明文が聞こえてきます。その説明文に関する1.～3.の質問文の答えとして最も適切なものを (A) ～ (D) より選び、その記号をマークしなさい。

1. What is the entrance fee for senior citizens?
   (A) $2
   (B) $4
   (C) $8
   (D) There is no fee.

   Ⓐ Ⓑ Ⓒ Ⓓ

2. On what days is Pioneer Park closed?
   (A) On weekends
   (B) On national holidays
   (C) On weekends and national holidays
   (D) On Christmas and New Years

   Ⓐ Ⓑ Ⓒ Ⓓ

3. Why is the caller most likely hearing this recorded message?
   (A) It is the weekend.
   (B) It is after museum hours.
   (C) The caller did not visit the website.
   (D) The caller is a senior citizen.

   Ⓐ Ⓑ Ⓒ Ⓓ

23

3. [PART 5] 短文穴埋め問題

Points

1. 時間順に。2. どのように避難すべきか？ 3. respected とのつながり。4. 見込み違い。5. inexpensive とマッチする副詞。

次の 1.～5. の英文について、------- に入れるべき最も適当なものをそれぞれ (A)～(D) より選び、その記号をマークしなさい。

1. The meetings with the Asian and African teams are scheduled for 10 AM and 4 PM, -------.
   (A) occasionally
   (B) inevitably
   (C) timely
   (D) respectively

   Ⓐ Ⓑ Ⓒ Ⓓ

2. All audience members must evacuate the theater ------- if the fire alarm sounds.
   (A) accidentally
   (B) briefly
   (C) immediately
   (D) primarily

   Ⓐ Ⓑ Ⓒ Ⓓ

3. Among all of our employees, the president is ------- respected by people who know him.
   (A) fully
   (B) annually
   (C) accurately
   (D) independently

   Ⓐ Ⓑ Ⓒ Ⓓ

4. The project was ------- estimated to cost $300,000, but the final expenses exceeded $600,000.
   (A) gradually
   (B) occasionally
   (C) initially
   (D) increasingly

   Ⓐ Ⓑ Ⓒ Ⓓ

5. A newly opened Chinese restaurant is popular for its wide selection of ------- inexpensive dishes.
   (A) effectively
   (B) closely
   (C) absolutely
   (D) relatively

   Ⓐ Ⓑ Ⓒ Ⓓ

Unit 4: 会話問題／説明文問題／短文穴埋め問題／長文穴埋め問題

4. [PART 6] 長文穴埋め問題

Points

作家リサ・ソープのシリーズ第4作に関する書評。1. 第4作をどうしたのか？　2. in his college days とのつながりは？　3. 空欄の前文には、これまでの作品と同様に…、と評価している。今回の作品は？　4. 1つ前の文でハッピーな展開を紹介しているが、この文は But で始まっている。

次の英文中の 1.~4. の空所に入れるべき最も適切なものをそれぞれ (A)~(D) の中から選び、その記号をマークしなさい。

Author Lisa Thorpe has just ---‑‑‑‑‑‑ her latest thriller, *Don't Look Back*, the
　　　　　　　　　　　　　　　1.
fourth book in her Jonathan Rock private detective series. This time Detective

Rock matches wits with a killer he ---‑‑‑‑‑ in his college days. Thorpe knows
　　　　　　　　　　　　　　　　　2.
how to keep the action moving and *Don't Look Back* has the same crisp dialog

and suspense as her other works. ---‑‑‑‑‑ Detective Rock falls in love! But if
　　　　　　　　　　　　　　　3.
you've read Thorpe before, you know she's not ---‑‑‑‑‑ happy endings. Read
　　　　　　　　　　　　　　　　　　　　　4.
Don't Look Back and see.

---

1. (A) begun 　　　(B) discussed 　　　(C) received 　　　(D) released

　　Ⓐ Ⓑ Ⓒ Ⓓ

2. (A) first killed 　　(B) first avoided 　(C) first met 　　(D) first wrote

　　Ⓐ Ⓑ Ⓒ Ⓓ

3. (A) But this time there is nothing new!
   (B) And this time it's the same!
   (C) But time there's something new!
   (D) This time she has no clue!

　　Ⓐ Ⓑ Ⓒ Ⓓ

4. (A) afraid of 　　(B) fooled by 　　(C) fond of 　　(D) free from

　　Ⓐ Ⓑ Ⓒ Ⓓ

Listening Section				Reading Section		
Part 1	Part 2	Part 3	Part 4	Part 5	Part 6	Part 7

Unit 5 応答問題／説明文問題／短文穴埋め問題／読解問題

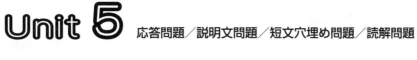

次の 1. ～ 7. の英文について、------- に入れるべき最も適当なものを (A), (B) より選びなさい。
（カッコ内はこの Unit 中の関連パートを表します。〈例〉Pt3 = Part 3）

1. ------- policies must be followed by all employees, including executives. (Pt4)
   (A) Corporate (B) Cooperated

2. Each ------- must submit an essay by the end of October. (Pt4)
   (A) application (B) candidate

3. We need to ------- wedding invitations to all of the guests by the beginning of next month. (Pt4)
   (A) distribute (B) attribute

4. Celebrities often ------- products on social media, but those aren't always good products. (Pt7)
   (A) criticize (B) endorse

5. The mayor announced her retirement and she named the deputy mayor as her -------. (Pt7)
   (A) descendent (B) successor

6. She is ------- with the project's success due to her exceptional leadership. (Pt7)
   (A) credit (B) credited

7. She has been asked to ------- the family business but has not yet made a decision. (Pt7)
   (A) take over (B) turn over

26

Unit 5: 応答問題／説明文問題／短文穴埋め問題／読解問題

1. [PART 2] 応答問題

Points

① 今回は質問文が「時間・期間」、「好き・嫌い」について尋ねている問題を扱う。
② 「時間」に関する質問文としては、What time ...?, When ...?, How long ...?, How soon ...? などの他に、Can you remember when ...?, How much longer ...? のようなバリエーションもある。
③ 「好き・嫌い」に関する質問文としては、Do you like ...?, How do you like ...?, Would you like ...? の他に、Do [Would] you prefer ...?, Are you interested in ...? などがある。

英文が聞こえ、その英文につづいて (A)(B)(C) 3 つの応答文が聞こえます。1.～5. の英文に対する最も適切な応答文を (A)～(C) の中から選び、その記号をマークしなさい。

15 1. Mark your answer on your sheet.

Ⓐ Ⓑ Ⓒ

2. Mark your answer on your sheet.

Ⓐ Ⓑ Ⓒ

3. Mark your answer on your sheet.

Ⓐ Ⓑ Ⓒ

4. Mark your answer on your sheet.

Ⓐ Ⓑ Ⓒ

5. Mark your answer on your sheet.

Ⓐ Ⓑ Ⓒ

27

2. [PART 4] 説明文問題

Points

質問文の先読みから、聞き取りのポイントをピックアップ
Questions 1 through 3: 何についてのアナウンスなのか？ どのようなジャーナリストを探しているのか？ 何語が必要とされているのか？ 政治に対する関心が必要な理由は？

1つの説明文が聞こえてきます。その説明文に関する 1.~3. の質問文の答えとして最も適切なものを (A)~(D) より選び、その記号をマークしなさい。

1. What type of journalist is Barney News looking for?
   (A) A free-lance journalist
   (B) A financial journalist
   (C) An online journalist
   (D) An editorialist

   Ⓐ   Ⓑ   Ⓒ   Ⓓ

2. What languages are necessary to get this position?
   (A) English and French
   (B) French and Spanish
   (C) Spanish and Japanese
   (D) English and Japanese

   Ⓐ   Ⓑ   Ⓒ   Ⓓ

3. Why must the multimedia producer be politically oriented?
   (A) The person must produce government news conferences.
   (B) The person must make audio interviews.
   (C) The person must distribute business news.
   (D) The person must deal with business experts.

   Ⓐ   Ⓑ   Ⓒ   Ⓓ

28

Unit 5: 応答問題／説明文問題／短文穴埋め問題／読解問題

3. [PART 5] 短文穴埋め問題

Points

1. file を目的語にする句動詞は？ 2. 副社長の飛行機が修理中なので。 3. 「(辞書などを)参照する」。
4. 「次々に」。 5. 「わざと、故意に」

次の 1.～5. の英文について、------- に入れるべき最も適当なものをそれぞれ (A)～(D) より選び、
その記号をマークしなさい。

1. Before you leave Ms. Simpson, please turn ------- the Huntly file to your supervisor.
   (A) down   (B) around
   (C) on   (D) in

   Ⓐ Ⓑ Ⓒ Ⓓ

2. The meeting scheduled for tomorrow morning will be put ------- because the vice president's plane is under repair.
   (A) on   (B) off
   (C) in   (D) to

   Ⓐ Ⓑ Ⓒ Ⓓ

3. Please ------- your notes for the homework assigned for the next class.
   (A) look in   (B) adapt to
   (C) keep on   (D) turn down

   Ⓐ Ⓑ Ⓒ Ⓓ

4. As a result of the final vote, our financial experts began to leave one after -------.
   (A) one   (B) another
   (C) themselves   (D) each

   Ⓐ Ⓑ Ⓒ Ⓓ

5. Did you do that ------- purpose in order to convince the stockholders that our shares will continue to go up?
   (A) with   (B) for
   (C) about   (D) on

   Ⓐ Ⓑ Ⓒ Ⓓ

29

4. [PART 7] 読解問題

Points

1つの文書
News article: トピックは市長選挙に関するレイモンド・リベラ市長の動向。1. 現市長が次回選挙に出ない理由は？ 2. 現市長は Karen Young 氏をどうしたいのか？

次の News article を読んで、1.~2. の答えとして最も適切なものを、それぞれ (A)~(D) の中から選び、その記号をマークしなさい。

Politics Briefs

Pleasant Hill (5 September) — Mayor Raymond Rivera of Pleasant Hill has announced he will not be seeking re-election to what would be a record fifth term. Mayor Rivera made the announcement at a city council meeting on Tuesday evening, where he also endorsed City Alderman Karen Young as his successor. The mayoral election is scheduled for this November and other candidates are expected to join the race. Mayor Rivera first won election in 2008 and is largely credited with attracting new businesses and jobs to Pleasant Hill. As to why he is not seeking re-election, Mayor Rivera cited his age. He explained he will turn 73 in August and that it was time to let younger people take over. As for his future plans, the Mayor reportedly said he hopes to go fishing more often.

1. What reason did the mayor give for not running for office again?
    (A) He doesn't think he can win a fifth term.
    (B) He has other plans for his future.
    (C) He will start a new business.
    (D) He thinks he is too old.

2. The word "successor" in line 5 is closest in meaning to
    (A) Someone who is successful
    (B) Someone who will come next
    (C) Someone who will be a candidate
    (D) Someone who is younger

	Listening Section			Reading Section		
Part 1	Part 2	Part 3	Part 4	Part 5	Part 6	Part 7

Unit 6 応答問題／説明文問題／短文穴埋め問題／読解問題

Warm-Up

次の 1.～7. の英文について、------- に入れるべき最も適当なものを (A), (B) より選びなさい。
(カッコ内はこの Unit 中の関連パートを表します。〈例〉Pt3 = Part 3)

1. The Spanish restaurant ------- the hotel concierge served delicious dishes. (Pt2)

   (A) recommending to   (B) recommended by

2. More orders than expected came in, so we hired ------- staff. (Pt2)

   (A) permanent   (B) temporary

3. I'd like to ------- you of our upcoming meeting at 4 PM. (Pt4)

   (A) remind   (B) remember

4. ------- in team sports as a child can improve communication skills. (Pt4)

   (A) Restriction   (B) Participation

5. According to the latest -------, 58% of the public approves of the new government. (Pt4)

   (A) survey   (B) intuition

6. All visitors must obtain an ------- pass from the main office. (Pt7)

   (A) admitted   (B) admittance

7. The order was not accepted because the credit card number was not -------. (Pt7)

   (A) invalid   (B) valid

31

1. [PART 2] 応答問題

Points

① 今回は質問文が「場所」、「確認など、何かの情報」について尋ねている問題を扱う。
②「場所」に関する質問文には、Where ...? の他に、(Can you) tell me where ...?, Do you know where ...? など、"where" が含まれる場合が多い。
③「確認など、何かの情報」に関する質問文としては、Is [Are, Was, Were] there ...?, 付加疑問文、Do [Did] you ...?, Is [Was] that ...?, Can we ...? など、疑問詞を使わない質問文が多い。

英文が聞こえ、その英文につづいて (A)(B)(C) 3 つの応答文が聞こえます。1.~5. の英文に対する最も適切な応答文を (A)～(C) の中から選び、その記号をマークしなさい。

1. Mark your answer on your sheet.

                     Ⓐ   Ⓑ   Ⓒ

2. Mark your answer on your sheet.

                     Ⓐ   Ⓑ   Ⓒ

3. Mark your answer on your sheet.

                     Ⓐ   Ⓑ   Ⓒ

4. Mark your answer on your sheet.

                     Ⓐ   Ⓑ   Ⓒ

5. Mark your answer on your sheet.

                     Ⓐ   Ⓑ   Ⓒ

Unit 6: 応答問題／説明文問題／短文穴埋め問題／読解問題

3. [PART 4] 説明文問題

Points

質問文の先読みから、聞き取りのポイントをピックアップ
Questions 1 through 3: 会議を早く終わりたい理由は？　授業評価の何が問題なのか？　先生が生徒に望むことは？

1つの説明文が聞こえてきます。その説明文に関する 1.～3. の質問文の答えとして最も適切なものを (A)～(D) より選び、その記号をマークしなさい。

1. Why does the speaker wish to finish early?

   (A) He wants to fill out a survey.

   (B) There is little to discuss.

   (C) There are no questions.

   (D) He has to go to class.

   Ⓐ　Ⓑ　Ⓒ　Ⓓ

2. What is the problem with the class evaluation surveys?

   (A) They can only be filled out by smartphone.

   (B) They have to be completed each term.

   (C) Not enough students are doing them.

   (D) They must be posted on the school website.

   Ⓐ　Ⓑ　Ⓒ　Ⓓ

3. What does the teacher suggest everyone do?

   (A) He suggests they adjourn early.

   (B) He suggests they leave in ten minutes.

   (C) He suggests they use class time for the surveys.

   (D) He suggests they fill out the surveys themselves.

   Ⓐ　Ⓑ　Ⓒ　Ⓓ

3. [PART 5] 短文穴埋め問題

Points

1. 形容詞の働き。2. 後には単数形の名詞。3. 時の一点、期限、期間？ 4. 意味上の主語の単複に注意。5. テレビ・コマーシャルができたら？

次の 1. ～ 5. の英文について、------- に入れるべき最も適当なものをそれぞれ (A)～(D) より選び、その記号をマークしなさい。

1. The ------- memo describes the corrections to be made on the report.
   (A) attached   (B) attach
   (C) attaching   (D) attaches

   Ⓐ Ⓑ Ⓒ Ⓓ

2. As ------- employee climbs the corporate ladder, there is more room at the bottom for failures.
   (A) other   (B) these
   (C) each   (D) ones

   Ⓐ Ⓑ Ⓒ Ⓓ

3. The client expects the contract to be signed ------- two weeks.
   (A) until   (B) within
   (C) by   (D) on

   Ⓐ Ⓑ Ⓒ Ⓓ

4. It takes a hard-working team of professionals to accomplish the job by -------.
   (A) they   (B) their
   (C) himself   (D) themselves

   Ⓐ Ⓑ Ⓒ Ⓓ

5. The marketing campaign will launch ------- the TV spot is ready.
   (A) so   (B) unless
   (C) when   (D) although

   Ⓐ Ⓑ Ⓒ Ⓓ

Unit 6: 応答問題／説明文問題／短文穴埋め問題／読解問題

4. [PART 7] 読解問題

Points

1つの文書
Coupon: トピックは、遊園地の入場クーポン券。1. 大人2、子供2、シニア1の合計金額。2. 持ち込み禁止は何？

次の Coupon を読んで、1.~2. の答えとして最も適切なものを、それぞれ (A)~(D) の中から選び、その記号をマークしなさい。

DISCOUNT COUPON FOR ADMISSION

This coupon is for admittance to Mobyland
and use of the Ahab Lagoon (water park), Thrilldome (indoor water park)

	REGULAR PRICE /	DISCOUNT PRICE
ADULTS (ages 13–60)	A$70.00	**$60.00 !**
CHILDREN (ages 7–12)	A$50.00	**$46.00 !**

NOTE : Infants, Senior Citizens (ages 2–6 / 61 and over) admitted at regular price $36.00

This coupon can be used to admit up to 5 people.
This coupon can only be used at Mobyland.
This coupon cannot be used for group discounts.

VALID UNTIL SEPT. 30TH 2026

Guests are not allowed to bring refreshments into the park.
Refreshments must be purchased inside the park.

35

1. How much would a family group of two adults and two children and one senior citizen pay to enter Mobyland using this coupon?
   (A) $212.00
   (B) $400.00
   (C) $272.00
   (D) $248.00

2. What can visitors NOT take into the park ?
   (A) Infants
   (B) Food and drink
   (C) Regular tickets
   (D) Diving gear

Listening Section				Reading Section		
Part 1	Part 2	Part 3	Part 4	Part 5	Part 6	Part 7

Unit 7 写真描写問題／会話問題／短文穴埋め問題／長文穴埋め問題

Warm-Up //

次の 1. ～ 7. の英文について、------- に入れるべき最も適当なものを (A), (B) より選びなさい。
(カッコ内はこの Unit 中の関連パートを表します。〈例〉Pt3 = Part 3)

1. Due to the earthquake, the ------- was delayed by three days. (Pt3)
   (A) recess
   (B) shipment

2. We have this T-shirt in XL size -------, but it will probably sell out within the next week. (Pt3)
   (A) in stock
   (B) out of stock

3. Every morning, Lin ------- at the coffee shop before going to work. (Pt3)
   (A) stops by
   (B) stops in

4. The family-owned bakery is a small-scale ------- that only opens three days a week. (Pt6)
   (A) operating
   (B) operation

5. Planting ------- species in your garden often helps support local wildlife. (Pt6)
   (A) threatened
   (B) native

6. People are now turning to ------- foods like ostrich meat instead of beef, pork, or chicken. (Pt6)
   (A) alternative
   (B) similar

7. Engineers tried to find the ------- of the problem but were unable to do so. (Pt6)
   (A) source
   (B) resource

1. [PART 1] 写真描写問題

Points
- 「人」が写っていない写真を取り扱う。このタイプの写真では、"モノが主語"になって、be placed, be installed, be cleaned, be opened, be watered などの受動態が散見される。
- また、"There are ..." の構文にも要注意。
- このタイプの写真でも、遠くに小さく見えるものや写真の片隅にある小物に関する描写は基本的にされない。

次の 1.〜 2. の写真について、それぞれの写真を説明する英文が 4 つ聞こえてきます。最も適切な英文を (A) 〜 (D) より選び、その記号をマークしなさい。

 No. 1

Ⓐ　Ⓑ　Ⓒ　Ⓓ

 No. 2

Ⓐ　Ⓑ　Ⓒ　Ⓓ

Unit 7: 写真描写問題／会話問題／短文穴埋め問題／長文穴埋め問題

2. [PART 3] 会話問題

Points

音変化を中心にピックアップ
＊ M-1 は男性の 1 番目、W-2 は、女性の 2 番目の発話を表します。
Questions 1 through 3 の会話: (M-1) in this section here (W-1) we're sold out (M-2) that has it (W-2) they're in stock
Questions 4 through 6 の会話: (M-1) I can't find the receipt (W-1) the one from the supply store (M-2) June 25th (W-2) going by there; stop in and ask

4 つの会話を聞き、それぞれの会話に関する 3 つの質問文の答えとして最も適切なものを (A) ～ (D) より選び、その記号をマークしなさい。

1. What is the man searching for?

    (A) Any place nearby
    (B) A kind of mustard
    (C) The store's mustard section
    (D) A different store branch

    Ⓐ Ⓑ Ⓒ Ⓓ

2. Why doesn't the store have what the man wants?

    (A) The shipment arrived only yesterday.
    (B) The shipment went to the next station.
    (C) The store has been sold.
    (D) The item is out of stock.

    Ⓐ Ⓑ Ⓒ Ⓓ

3. What does the woman suggest that the man do?

    (A) She suggests he ask his wife.
    (B) She suggests he buy some stock.
    (C) She suggests checking at a different branch.
    (D) She suggests he come back next week.

    Ⓐ Ⓑ Ⓒ Ⓓ

22. 4. Where does this conversation most likely take place?
    (A) In the speakers' office
    (B) Near a cash register
    (C) At a shop with a fax service
    (D) Somewhere in the supply store

    Ⓐ Ⓑ Ⓒ Ⓓ

5. What happened on June 25th?
    (A) They got a fax from Eric.
    (B) They went to a copy shop.
    (C) They bought some supplies.
    (D) They gave a customer a receipt.

    Ⓐ Ⓑ Ⓒ Ⓓ

6. What does the woman offer to do?
    (A) Look for the receipt
    (B) Call Eric
    (C) Get another receipt
    (D) Fax it to the man

    Ⓐ Ⓑ Ⓒ Ⓓ

Unit 7: 写真描写問題／会話問題／短文穴埋め問題／長文穴埋め問題

3. [PART 5] 短文穴埋め問題

Points

1. banker が扱う書類。2. 形容詞形は？ 3. 名詞を修飾する形容詞。4. 「It is ... to 不定詞」の構文。
5. 冠詞なしでも使える形容詞。

次の 1.～5. の英文について、------- に入れるべき最も適切なものをそれぞれ (A)～(D) の中から
選び、その記号をマークしなさい。

1. Mr. Ruskin is a banker whose job routinely involves ------- documents.
   (A) financial   (B) preferential
   (C) sacrificial   (D) parental

   Ⓐ Ⓑ Ⓒ Ⓓ

2. ------- planning is essential for a successful presentation.
   (A) Thoughtfully   (B) Thought
   (C) Thoughtful   (D) Thinking

   Ⓐ Ⓑ Ⓒ Ⓓ

3. Mr. Cummings wearily returned from the clinic late in the afternoon and told
   us that he had had a ------- physical exam.
   (A) complete   (B) worth
   (C) contrary   (D) liable

   Ⓐ Ⓑ Ⓒ Ⓓ

4. It is ------- to offer a high salary to secure outstandingly skilled professionals.
   (A) reasonably   (B) reasoned
   (C) reasonable   (D) reason

   Ⓐ Ⓑ Ⓒ Ⓓ

5. Any company that plans to open ------- businesses in that small town will
   probably fail.
   (A) solitary   (B) alone
   (C) same   (D) similar

   Ⓐ Ⓑ Ⓒ Ⓓ

41

4. [PART 6] 長文穴埋め問題

> **Points**
>
> トピックは、アマゾン原産のビタミンCが世界一豊富な果物"カムカム"。1. than any other に注目。2.「大規模栽培プロジェクトに着手するという計画」3. 空欄の前文 "the camu camu is attracting renewed interest" と空欄以下の文中 "... will help save these wild trees" とのつながりは？ 4. ビタミンC 含有量の言い換え。

次の英文中の1.~4.の空所に入れるべき最も適切なものをそれぞれ (A)~(D) の中から選び、その記号をマークしなさい。

AE Health Foods to Grow Camu Camu on a Large Scale

The camu camu, a cherry-like fruit from the Amazon, is -------- in Vitamin C than any other fruit in the world. As such, AE Health Foods Company announced Thursday their plan -------- a large-scale operation to grow the fruit in the Amazon Basin, the native home of the small tree.

With today's increased awareness in healthy eating and the search for alternative foods, the camu camu is attracting renewed interest. -------- According to AE spokesperson Bill Watts, the food company hopes their plantation will help save these wild trees, which have long been used as source of food by the native tribes of Brazil and Peru.

The camu camu contains about 2800 mg of Vitamin C per 100 g of fruit, or almost 60 times the -------- of oranges.

---

1. (A) richer
   (B) richest
   (C) more richly
   (D) most richly

42

Unit 7: 写真描写問題／会話問題／短文穴埋め問題／長文穴埋め問題

2. (A) start

(B) starting

(C) started

(D) to start

Ⓐ Ⓑ Ⓒ Ⓓ

3. (A) And healthy eating starts with learning new ways to eat.

(B) And we are unfamiliar with alternative foods.

(C) But that demand has put stress on the wild plant, endangering its existence.

(D) But there is an endless supply of very cheap labor.

Ⓐ Ⓑ Ⓒ Ⓓ

4. (A) concentration

(B) dilution

(C) suspension

(D) retention

Ⓐ Ⓑ Ⓒ Ⓓ

43

	Listening Section			Reading Section		
Part 1	Part 2	Part 3	Part 4	Part 5	Part 6	Part 7

Unit 8 応答問題／会話問題／説明文問題／読解問題

𝑾arm-Up //

次の 1. ～ 8. の英文について、------- に入れるべき最も適当なものを (A), (B) より選びなさい。
（カッコ内はこの Unit 中の関連パートを表します。〈例〉Pt3 = Part 3）

1. Janet invited me to see a horror movie, but I don't actually ------- horror films. (Pt3)
   (A) look over   (B) care for

2. The earthquake caused extensive damage to buildings, but ------- were reported. (Pt4)
   (A) no injuries   (B) many injuries

3. Usually, there's little ------- on the roads during weekdays, but today it was terrible. (Pt4)
   (A) traffic   (B) trail

4. The show started later than scheduled because of ------- at the concert entrance. (Pt4)
   (A) conservation   (B) congestion

5. Even if it rains tomorrow morning, there is no ------- plan. (Pt7)
   (A) alternate   (B) detailed

6. Artificial intelligence is expected to soon ------- several industries. (Pt7)
   (A) dominating   (B) dominate

7. Many customers ------- this product as environmentally friendly. (Pt7)
   (A) are rated   (B) rate

8. The software is designed to ------- and block fake news from websites. (Pt7)
   (A) detect   (B) overlook

44

Unit 8: 応答問題／会話問題／説明文問題／読解問題

1. [PART 2] 応答問題

Points

① 今回は質問文が「原因・理由」「経験」「方法・手段」を表す問題を扱う。
② 「原因・理由」を尋ねる質問文としては、Why ...? 以外に Do you know why ...? もある。
③ 「経験」を尋ねる質問文としては、Have you ...? がよく使われる。
④ 「方法・手段」を尋ねる質問文としては、How did [do] you ...?, How can I [you] ...? が多い。

英文が聞こえ、その英文につづいて (A)(B)(C) 3 つの応答文が聞こえます。1.~5. の英文に対する最も適切な応答文を (A)~(C) の中から選び、その記号をマークしなさい。

23 1. Mark your answer on your sheet.

Ⓐ　Ⓑ　Ⓒ

2. Mark your answer on your sheet.

Ⓐ　Ⓑ　Ⓒ

3. Mark your answer on your sheet.

Ⓐ　Ⓑ　Ⓒ

4. Mark your answer on your sheet.

Ⓐ　Ⓑ　Ⓒ

5. Mark your answer on your sheet.

Ⓐ　Ⓑ　Ⓒ

45

2. [PART 3] 会話問題

> **Points**
>
> 音変化を中心にピックアップ
> Questions 1 through 3: 話者は給仕と男女の客。レストランでの会話。音変化としては、what comes with your; come with a; I don't care for; listed inside the menu

次の会話を聞き、それぞれの会話に関する3つの質問文の答えとして最も適切なものを (A) ～ (D) より選び、その記号をマークしなさい。

 1. What comes with the lunch specials?
   - (A) Fries
   - (B) A grilled cheese sandwich
   - (C) Salad and soup
   - (D) Clam chowder

2. Why doesn't the man want a lunch special?
   - (A) He wants fries.
   - (B) He dislikes clam chowder
   - (C) He isn't ready to order.
   - (D) He doesn't like soup.

Ⓐ Ⓑ Ⓒ Ⓓ

3. Where are drinks listed in the menu?
   - (A) On the back cover
   - (B) Inside the back cover
   - (C) Outside the back cover
   - (D) Inside the front cover.

3. [PART 4] 説明文問題

Points

質問文の先読みから、聞き取りのポイントをピックアップ
Questions 1 through 3: 誰が誰に発している情報なのか？ 道路で起きたこと、交通の状態、道路で処理をしているのは誰か？

1つの説明文が聞こえてきます。その説明文に関する1.～3.の質問文の答えとして最も適切なものを(A)～(D)より選び、その記号をマークしなさい。

1. What can be used as an alternate route?
    (A) Richmond Boulevard
    (B) Route 66
    (C) Huron Road
    (D) Superior Avenue

    Ⓐ Ⓑ Ⓒ Ⓓ

2. What does the reporter say about the traffic conditions?
    (A) Light traffic
    (B) Light to moderate traffic
    (C) Moderate traffic
    (D) Moderate to heavy traffic

    Ⓐ Ⓑ Ⓒ Ⓓ

3. Who is dealing with the farm animals?
    (A) Tod Warner
    (B) State Highway Patrol officers
    (C) WEWS traffic personnel
    (D) Mr. Richmond

    Ⓐ Ⓑ Ⓒ Ⓓ

4. [PART 7] 読解問題

> **Points**
>
> 1つの文書
> 設問 1–2: ある Web page に関する問題。トピックは、AI。AI が作成したコンテンツを AI が分析・判定するというサイト。1. ユーザーが利用するためには？ 2. 利用料は？

次の Web page を読んで、1.～2. の答えとして最も適切なものを、それぞれ (A) ～ (D) の中から選び、その記号をマークしなさい。

---

https://www.aidetective.com/home

AI Detective!

In only a short time, AI-generated texts and images have come to dominate the world's media. Yet, responsible people need to know! Was the document just received written by a human being? Or was it instead AI-created? **AI Detective** will find the truth!

AI Detective rates as one of the most accurate websites for detecting artificial intelligence content. Trust **AI Detective** to give you a clear profile of all texts and images received.

Just upload the text or image you wish to check into the space below. **AI Detective** will analyze the content within seconds.

Each website visitor receives two free uploads per day. For unlimited uploads and more detailed analysis, select from our premium packages in the menu bar. Prices start from $10.00 a month.

1. What must website visitors do in order to learn more about a suspicious text?
   (A) They need to select from the website's premium packages.
   (B) They need to upload the text onto the AI Detective website.
   (C) They need to present a clear profile of the text.
   (D) They need to trust AI Detective.

   Ⓐ Ⓑ Ⓒ Ⓓ

2. How much will it cost visitors to have a text or image analyzed?
   (A) They need to purchase a premium package.
   (B) The minimum fee is $10.00 a month.
   (C) A single upload is free.
   (D) They need to consult the menu bar.

   Ⓐ Ⓑ Ⓒ Ⓓ

Listening Section				Reading Section		
Part 1	Part 2	Part 3	Part 4	Part 5	Part 6	Part 7

Unit 9 応答問題／会話問題／説明文問題／読解問題

Warm-Up

次の 1. ～ 8. の英文について、------- に入れるべき最も適当なものを (A), (B) より選びなさい。
（カッコ内はこの Unit 中の関連パートを表します。〈例〉Pt3 = Part 3）

1. The manager had several questions ------- the first quarter sales report. (Pt4)
   (A) in regard to
   (B) regarding to

2. Jennifer is ------- a traffic jam and will be late for the meeting. (Pt4)
   (A) stuck in
   (B) stuck to

3. The highway is ------- due to a fire nearby. (Pt4)
   (A) flowed down
   (B) backed up

4. I hope my early arrival doesn't cause you any -------. (Pt4)
   (A) convenience
   (B) inconvenience

5. ------- the typhoon, the outdoor concert was postponed. (Pt7)
   (A) Instead of
   (B) Owing to

6. Kevin noticed some hidden ------- on his receipt. (Pt7)
   (A) charges
   (B) bills

7. I enjoy many genres of music, but jazz, -------, relaxes me. (Pt7)
   (A) in particular
   (B) in turn

8. To stay successful in today's ------- marketplace, companies must continually reassess their market strategies. (Pt7)
   (A) indifferent
   (B) competitive

50

Unit 9: 応答問題／会話問題／説明文問題／読解問題

1. [PART 2] 応答問題

Points

① 今回は質問文が「予定」「義務・必要」を表す問題、また、質問文形式ではなく平叙文に対する応答を問う問題を扱う。

② 「予定」を尋ねる質問文には、"be + ...ing" の形を含むものが多く、Is ... ...ing ...?, We're ...ing ..., aren't we?, You're ...ing ..., aren't you?, Will ... be ...ing ..., or ...? など多様である。

③ 「義務・必要」を表す質問文としては、Should ...?, Shouldn't ...? などの他に、You should ..., We should ... などの平叙文が第 1 文となるパターンも多い。また、should の代わりに need to *do* を使った平叙文もある。

英文が聞こえ、その英文につづいて (A)(B)(C) 3 つの応答文が聞こえます。1.～5. の英文に対する最も適切な応答文を (A)～(C) の中から選び、その記号をマークしなさい。

26　1. Mark your answer on your sheet.

Ⓐ　Ⓑ　Ⓒ

2. Mark your answer on your sheet.

Ⓐ　Ⓑ　Ⓒ

3. Mark your answer on your sheet.

Ⓐ　Ⓑ　Ⓒ

4. Mark your answer on your sheet.

Ⓐ　Ⓑ　Ⓒ

5. Mark your answer on your sheet.

Ⓐ　Ⓑ　Ⓒ

51

2. [PART 3] 会話問題

Points

2 人の会話：図表を見て答える設問を含む問題
Questions 1 through 3: ホテルのフロントでの会話。音変化としては、Here is your hotel key; with your bags; remind you; served in the Dining Hall

次の会話を聞き、それぞれの会話に関する 3 つの質問文の答えとして最も適切なものを (A) ～ (D) より選び、その記号をマークしなさい。

```
                        Hotel Directory
1F:         Lobby
2F:         Dining Hall
3F–9F:      Hotel Rooms
10F:        Suite Rooms
11F:        Restaurants – Great Wall (Chinese)
                         & Mi Casa (Italian)
```

27 1. What did the man give to the woman?

(A) His bags   (B) A hotel key
(C) A bellhop   (D) A hotel directory

Ⓐ Ⓑ Ⓒ Ⓓ

2. 2. What is NOT necessary for the woman?

(A) Breakfast at the hotel   (B) Bags to bring to the hotel
(C) The help of a bellhop   (D) A meal at a restaurant

Ⓐ Ⓑ Ⓒ Ⓓ

3. Look at the graphic. Where can the woman go to have breakfast at the hotel?

(A) 2nd floor   (B) 1st floor
(C) 11th floor   (D) 2nd floor or 11th floor

Ⓐ Ⓑ Ⓒ Ⓓ

Unit 9: 応答問題／会話問題／説明文問題／読解問題

3. [PART 4] 説明文問題

Points

質問文の先読みから、聞き取りのポイントをピックアップ
Questions 1 through 3: 誰が誰に発している情報なのか？ 電話のトピックの中心は何か？ 話者の目的は何か？ 何か事故が起きたらしいが…。話者が次に行いそうなアクションは？

1つの説明文が聞こえてきます。その説明文に関する 1.～3. の質問文の答えとして最も適切なものを (A)～(D) より選び、その記号をマークしなさい。

1. What is the purpose of this call?

    (A) To advertise air conditioning units
    (B) To confirm the delivery time for a purchase
    (C) To tell about a traffic accident on the freeway
    (D) To apologize for being late

    Ⓐ　Ⓑ　Ⓒ　Ⓓ

2. What does the speaker imply when he says "there was some sort of accident"?

    (A) The delivery truck had an accident.
    (B) He is not sure what happened exactly.
    (C) There were assorted troubles.
    (D) The accident was of a terrible sort.

    Ⓐ　Ⓑ　Ⓒ　Ⓓ

3. What will the speaker do next to assist the listener?

    (A) Call again
    (B) Arrive as early as possible
    (C) Apologize once more
    (D) Avoid traffic jams

    Ⓐ　Ⓑ　Ⓒ　Ⓓ

4. [PART 7] 読解問題

Points

1つの文書
設問 1–2: Letter: トピックは、お茶の値上げの通知。1. 差出人の社名は第1行目に。
2. 本文第1行目にキーワードが。

次の Letter を読んで、1.～2. の答えとして最も適切なものを、それぞれ (A)～(D) の中から選び、その記号をマークしなさい。

Eastern Tea Wholesale
1-21 Tomihisa-Cho, Shinjuku-Ku, Tokyo 162-0067
Phone: 03-3359-3967

To our valued customers:
Owing to the recent steep rise in trans-Pacific shipping and terminal handling charges, we have found it necessary to increase our prices on East Asian teas. Shipping rates in particular, as we are sure you are aware, are one of the chief determining factors in tea prices.

We ask you to understand that our prices have been raised no higher than necessary, and are still highly competitive in view of current market trends.

We wish to assure you that we will continue to pursue our goal of providing the finest quality at the best price for our customers.

Sincerely,

Nyoman Gede
Nyoman Gede

54

Unit 9: 応答問題／会話問題／説明文問題／読解問題

1. What can be said about the writer of this letter?

   (A) He has increased shipping and handling charges.

   (B) He owns a fleet of ships.

   (C) He is a tea exporter.

   (D) He is negotiating tea prices.

   Ⓐ　Ⓑ　Ⓒ　Ⓓ

2. Where is this letter most probably being sent?

   (A) To India

   (B) To the United States

   (C) To Europe

   (D) To Africa

   Ⓐ　Ⓑ　Ⓒ　Ⓓ

	Listening Section			Reading Section		
Part 1	Part 2	Part 3	Part 4	Part 5	Part 6	Part 7

Unit 10 応答問題／会話問題／説明文問題／読解問題

Warm-Up

次の 1.～10. の英文について、------- に入れるべき最も適当なものを (A), (B) より選びなさい。
（カッコ内はこの Unit 中の関連パートを表します。〈例〉Pt3 = Part 3）

1. My gym membership is set to ------- at the weekend, so I need to renew it soon. (Pt2)
   (A) extend
   (B) expire

2. The meeting ------- will be sent to all participants two weeks in advance. (Pt3)
   (A) facilities
   (B) agenda

3. The CEO's ------- at the annual meeting highlighted the company's future goals. (Pt3)
   (A) remarked
   (B) remarks

4. After the keynote speech, there was ------- for lunch. (Pt3)
   (A) an adjournment
   (B) a completion

5. I need to free up storage space by ------- old files on my computer. (Pt3)
   (A) getting rid of
   (B) looking up on

6. The two companies ------- the terms of the deal before signing. (Pt4)
   (A) called upon
   (B) agreed upon

7. The University's ------- year runs from April 1 to March 31, aligned with the academic calendar. (Pt4)
   (A) following
   (B) fiscal

8. All ------- must possess a bachelor's degree in economics and have a minimum of six months of work experience. (Pt7)
   (A) candidates
   (B) applications

56

Unit 10: 応答問題／会話問題／説明文問題／読解問題

9. The company has announced a ------- for a graphic designer for its website. (Pt7)

   (A) vacancy   (B) launch

10. I have a new ------- at work that involves attending a trade fair in Amsterdam. (Pt7)

   (A) assessment   (B) assignment

1. [PART 2] 応答問題

Points

① 今回はその他の頻出する質問文を取り扱う。
② Who ...?, Which ...?, How ...? と付加疑問文のほか、Unit 9 でも取り上げたが、質問文の代わりに平叙文が第 1 文となっている問題も取り扱う。

英文が聞こえ、その英文につづいて (A)(B)(C) 3 つの応答文が聞こえます。1.～5. の英文に対する最も適切な応答文を (A)～(C) の中から選び、その記号をマークしなさい。

(29) 1. Mark your answer on your sheet.

                                                  Ⓐ Ⓑ Ⓒ

2. Mark your answer on your sheet.

                                                  Ⓐ Ⓑ Ⓒ

3. Mark your answer on your sheet.

                                                  Ⓐ Ⓑ Ⓒ

4. Mark your answer on your sheet.

                                                  Ⓐ Ⓑ Ⓒ

5. Mark your answer on your sheet.

                                                  Ⓐ Ⓑ Ⓒ

2. [PART 3] 会話問題

> **Points**
> 2人の会話：図表に関する設問を含む問題
> Questions 1 through 3: 会議出席者同士の会話。音変化としては、time to check in; begin in twenty minutes; filling up; get a seat; get rid of this bag; set up during lunch time

次の会話を聞き、それぞれの会話に関する3つの質問文の答えとして最も適切なものを (A) ～ (D) より選び、その記号をマークしなさい。

2024 Medical Technicians Conference Agenda

Friday, June 7th

8:00 – 9:00	Registration
9:00 – 9:30	Opening Remarks
9:30 – 10:00	Keynote Address by Dr. Irving Warren of Ace Institute
10:00 – 10:30	Coffee Break (Coffee and tea will be served in the registration lobby)
10:30 – 12:00	Panel Discussion on Elderly Patient Care, moderated by Dr. Sharon Itoh of Avery Technology
12:00 – 2:00	Lunch Break
2:00 – 3:30	Workshop 1 (See the accompanying sheet for room numbers)
4:00 – 5:30	Workshop 2 (See the accompanying sheet for room numbers)

---

 1. Where is this conversation most likely taking place?

    (A) In the man's hotel   (B) At the registration desk
    (C) In the meeting hall   (D) In a workshop room

2. Why does the man hope to check-in at his hotel soon?

    (A) It is just across the street.
    (B) He is leading one of the workshops
    (C) The conference will be starting in a moment.
    (D) He wants to put away his luggage.

Unit 10: 応答問題／会話問題／説明文問題／読解問題

3. Look at the Graphic. What time will the man be leading his workshop?
   (A) At 2:00 (B) At 3:30 (C) At 4:00 (D) At 5:30

   Ⓐ Ⓑ Ⓒ Ⓓ

3. [PART 4] 説明文問題

Points

質問文の先読みから、聞き取りのポイントをピックアップ
Questions 1 through 3: どのような会議に関するインフォメーションなのか？ 話者が伝えている "ask the advertising department to look at our packaging" ということが示唆することは？ 今四半期に値上げを行わない理由は？

1つの説明文が聞こえてきます。その説明文に関する 1.～3. の質問文の答えとして最も適切なものを (A)～(D) より選び、その記号をマークしなさい。

1. What kind of meeting was this?
   (A) A campaign meeting
   (B) A meeting for representatives of the main office
   (C) A meeting for possible distributors
   (D) A sales meeting

   Ⓐ Ⓑ Ⓒ Ⓓ

2. What does the speaker imply when he says, "ask the advertising department to look at our packaging"?
   (A) Some representatives want to review a budget proposal.
   (B) Some representatives need to clarify a statement about advertising.
   (C) Some representatives want the advertising department to review the packaging.
   (D) Some representatives are thinking of discussing a package design.

   Ⓐ Ⓑ Ⓒ Ⓓ

3. Why none of the prices will be increased for this fiscal quarter?
   (A) To keep the top share in the market
   (B) To maintain sales for three months
   (C) To win the competition in the market
   (D) To prepare for the winter campaigns

   Ⓐ Ⓑ Ⓒ Ⓓ

4. [PART 7] 読解問題

Points

1つの文書
設問 1–3: Advertisement: トピックは、出版社の求人広告。3. どのような職種の人材募集か？
4. 設問中の Also がキーワード。5. 文書の後半に注目。

次の Advertisement を読んで、問い 1.~3. の答えとして最も適切なものを、それぞれ (A)~(D) の中から選び、その記号をマークしなさい。

Job Opportunity for Journalist

INVESTMENT MONTHLY

bureau in Sofia is seeking a journalist to join its team to cover either the Bulgarian financial industry or the agricultural sector (depending on staff movements). — [1] —. The ideal candidate will be fluent in English, have writing experience, and a good knowledge of Bulgarian. — [2] —. The current job vacancy is for a local staff position writing for the magazine, however, it offers potential for promotion onto staff in different offices across the global Investment Monthly network at a later date. — [3] —. The work assignment is for six months. — [4] —. Applications should be sent by July 23rd to: Igor Bever, Investment Monthly Editorial, 3 Berezovsky Prospekt, Sofia.

---

1. Where would this advertisement most probably appear?
   (A) In a farmers' gazette
   (B) In a financial periodical
   (C) In a party-political pamphlet
   (D) In a tourist guidebook

   Ⓐ Ⓑ Ⓒ Ⓓ

2. In which of the positions marked [1], [2], [3], and [4] does the following sentence best belong?
   "Also, they should have a keen interest in business and finance and, above all, should be very enthusiastic and adaptable."
   (A) [1]   (B) [2]   (C) [3]   (D) [4]

   Ⓐ Ⓑ Ⓒ Ⓓ

Unit 10: 応答問題／会話問題／説明文問題／読解問題

3. What should an interested candidate do?

(A) Write an article

(B) Submit new financial plans

(C) Arrange for an interview

(D) Send an application

Ⓐ　Ⓑ　Ⓒ　Ⓓ

Listening Section				Reading Section		
Part 1	Part 2	Part 3	**Part 4**	Part 5	Part 6	Part 7

Unit 11 説明文問題／読解問題

Warm-Up

次の 1. ～ 10. の英文について、------- に入れるべき最も適当なものを (A), (B) より選びなさい。
（カッコ内はこの Unit 中の関連パートを表します。〈例〉Pt3 = Part 3）

1. I found a nice new restaurant ------- to the office. Would you like to go for lunch? (Pt4)
    (A) close
    (B) closing

2. Using trains instead of cars ------- reducing carbon dioxide levels in the atmosphere. (Pt7)
    (A) results from
    (B) contributes to

3. Power Tech is ------- expand its operations in Africa next year. (Pt7)
    (A) looking for
    (B) looking to

4. There is an increasing ------- on promoting compliance awareness in the workplace. (Pt7)
    (A) emphasis
    (B) indifference

5. The ------- of young workers in the restaurant industry has driven up salaries and benefits. (Pt7)
    (A) scarcity
    (B) surplus

6. International cooperation on climate change is crucial for global ------- and peace. (Pt7)
    (A) hardship
    (B) prosperity

7. ------- endurance, he is one of the best players on the team. (Pt7)
    (A) On account of
    (B) In terms of

8. Investing in stocks can ------- significant gains over time, but it also carries certain risks. (Pt7)

   (A) drop   (B) generate

9. The company's annual ------- increased by 12% last year. (Pt7)

   (A) returns   (B) returning

10. Lowering taxes can ------- many businesses by increasing their profitability. (Pt7)

    (A) benefit   (B) distress

1. [PART 4] 説明文問題

> **Points**
>
> 質問文の先読みから、聞き取りのポイントをピックアップ
> Questions 1 through 3: 何についてのアナウンスなのか？ 15 分で店が閉まるということが示唆していることは？ アナウンスの最後に何を言っているか？
> Questions 4 through 6: 荷物について言われていることは？ 「あと 10 分だけ」が示唆していることは？ 乗客が搭乗するときに求められていることは？

2 つの説明文が聞こえてきます。その説明文に関する 1.～6. の質問文の答えとして最も適切なものを (A)～(D) より選び、その記号をマークしなさい。

1. What is this announcement mainly about?
   (A) Tomorrow's store schedule   (B) The store's back door
   (C) The store closing   (D) The store's prices

   Ⓐ Ⓑ Ⓒ Ⓓ

2. What does the speaker imply when she says, "We will be closing in fifteen minutes"?
   (A) Frank wants the shoppers to collect final payments.
   (B) Frank is requesting the shoppers to finish their shopping soon.
   (C) The shoppers should hold some items right now.
   (D) The shoppers should not try a different product.

   Ⓐ Ⓑ Ⓒ Ⓓ

3. What does the speaker do toward the end of the announcement?
   (A) Ask shoppers to hurry again
   (B) Call for the manager
   (C) Talk about store items
   (D) Say thank you again

   Ⓐ Ⓑ Ⓒ Ⓓ

4. What does the speaker say about bags?
   (A) They can be picked up at Gate 12B.
   (B) There is a limit to the number of carry-ons.
   (C) They have found some lost ones.
   (D) All of them must be checked.

   Ⓐ Ⓑ Ⓒ Ⓓ

5. What does the speaker imply when she says, "They should only be another ten minutes"?
   (A) Passengers need ten minutes to update.
   (B) Passengers don't have to wait too long.
   (C) The cleaning crew takes more time than expected.
   (D) The cleaning crew will arrive by a certain time.

   Ⓐ Ⓑ Ⓒ Ⓓ

6. What does the speaker tell the listeners to do when boarding?
   (A) Hand their boarding passes to the staff
   (B) Wait for ten minutes
   (C) Check in their bags
   (D) Go to Gate 12B

   Ⓐ Ⓑ Ⓒ Ⓓ

Unit 11: 説明文問題／読解問題

2. [PART 7] 読解問題

Points

2つの文書
Article: トピックは、急速に成長する環境ビジネス。E-mail: 記事を読んだ人が記事の編集者へ出したメール。
1. Article の第3段落にキーがある。2. Article の第4段落にキーがある。3. E-mail の第1段落後半にキーがある。4. E-mail の第2段落前半にキーがある。5. Article の第3段落にキーがある。

次の Article と E-mail を読んで、1.~5. の答えとして最も適切なものをそれぞれ (A)~(D) の中より選び、その記号をマークしなさい。

Environmental Business Taking off

Environmental business is becoming big business. Several factors have contributed to the growth of environment-friendly, or so-called 'green', technologies and industries. Some investors and corporations, especially in the power sector, appear to be taking notice.

One company looking to take advantage of this growth is China-based Power Tech, whose CEO Frank Wong announced at the company's shareholder meeting last week that the power company has shifted emphasis to efforts in the natural energy market and will gradually be spinning off the petroleum processing component of its business.

"As a company we are about making money, and this direction will increase our presence in the fast-growing natural power sector. It will be good for investors and developing countries, such as my native China."

One factor behind this trend is scarcity of resources. Another is rising incomes, especially in Asia, where two-thirds of the global population lives. Economic concerns are being joined by environmental concerns as nations work to achieve prosperity and a clean environment. Clearly, some companies see this as a great business opportunity.

65

To:	Editors of Today News Service <editor@todaynewsservice.com>
From:	Will J. Clark <wjclark@sharehold.com>
Date:	Ferbruary 9
Subject:	Article

I was excited to read about the comments by CEO Frank Wong about the new direction of Power Tech. As a shareholder of the company, I was even more excited that his comments drove up the share price to a high for the year. It is about time that society recognized the potential profit of natural, or 'green', power. I have heard analysts say that solar power is replacing hydro and coal power in terms of growth for years. Now this seems to be becoming a reality.

It is a good feeling to be able to be connected to a company that is generating not only great returns, but also helping societies. In this way, it seems that this is an example of how corporations, citizens and developing countries can benefit at the same time. I wouldn't mind if Power Tech stock splits again in the near future either!
Keep up the good work.

Sincerely yours,
Will J. Clark

1. What did Mr. Wong announce at the meeting?
   (A) The number of investors will increase.
   (B) The petroleum products will increase.
   (C) Power Tech will be more profitable.
   (D) The energy market in China will fall.

   Ⓐ Ⓑ Ⓒ Ⓓ

2. What is a reason given for the growth in the natural power sector?
   (A) New technologies   (B) Resource shortage
   (C) Climate change   (D) Water pollution

Unit 11: 説明文問題／読解問題

3. What is a technology that the reader feels confident will be profitable?

(A) Hydro power

(B) Coal power

(C) Solar power

(D) Nuclear power

Ⓐ Ⓑ Ⓒ Ⓓ

4. Who does the reader think stands to benefit from environmental technology?

(A) Reporters and editors

(B) Corporations and citizens

(C) Non-government organizations and students

(D) Politicians and bureaucrats

Ⓐ Ⓑ Ⓒ Ⓓ

5. Where can it be inferred that growth is NOT expected to be especially strong in the natural power industry?

(A) China

(B) Developing countries

(C) Countries except China

(D) Industrialized nations

Ⓐ Ⓑ Ⓒ Ⓓ

67

Listening Section				Reading Section		
Part 1	Part 2	Part 3	**Part 4**	Part 5	Part 6	**Part 7**

Unit 12 説明文問題／読解問題

Warm-Up

次の 1. ～ 10. の英文について、------- に入れるべき最も適当なものを (A), (B) より選びなさい。
(カッコ内はこの Unit 中の関連パートを表します。〈例〉Pt3 = Part 3)

1. The hotel offers a range of recreational ------- including a swimming pool and gym. (Pt4)
   (A) facilities
   (B) institutions

2. The marathon runners are ------- start the race. (Pt4)
   (A) getting ready to
   (B) getting used to

3. His tie ------- perfectly with his suit and shirt. (Pt7)
   (A) matching
   (B) matches

4. My three-year-old son can go to the bathroom and come back -------. (Pt7)
   (A) in his place
   (B) on his own

5. The October trip ------- includes many tourist attractions and historical sites. (Pt7)
   (A) attendee
   (B) itinerary

6. Many companies offer health insurance ------- retirement benefits. (Pt7)
   (A) as well as
   (B) as good as

7. This version of the tablet is the most ------- one we've released so far. (Pt7)
   (A) completing
   (B) complete

8. Doctors had to perform emergency ------- to save the lives of hurricane victims. (Pt7)
   (A) surgery
   (B) repairs

68

9. Jim ------- understood what Sue was saying, but he pretended not to understand. (Pt7)
   (A) sort of   (B) in turn

10. It's always crucial to keep the deadline in ------- when working on your project. (Pt7)
    (A) heart   (B) mind

1. [PART 4] 説明文問題

Points

質問文の先読みから、聞き取りのポイントをピックアップ
Questions 1 through 3: アナウンスの目的は？ 地下鉄で来るとどんな利点がある？ 2番目に近い地下鉄の駅はどこに？

1つの説明文が聞こえてきます。その説明文と地図に関する1.～3.の質問文の答えとして最も適切なものを(A)～(D)より選び、その記号をマークしなさい。

1. What is the purpose of this announcement?
    (A) To encourage people to join Patty's Gym
    (B) To give directions to the newest branch of Patty's Gym
    (C) To help busy people save time
    (D) To encourage people to come by subway and not by car

    Ⓐ Ⓑ Ⓒ Ⓓ

2. Why would it be better to arrive by subway and then to walk?
    (A) Visitors can view the Snake River.
    (B) Visitors can exercise by walking.
    (C) The new branch is easy to find.
    (D) There are few places to park a car.

    Ⓐ Ⓑ Ⓒ Ⓓ

3. Look at the graphic. Where is the second closest subway exit for the Bedford branch of Patty's Gym?
    (A) North of the Snake River and near Lake Larson on Western Avenue
    (B) East of Oak Point Avenue by the Snake River
    (C) Near the corner of Ashton Street and Western Avenue
    (D) On Everly Road, north of Bedford.

    Ⓐ Ⓑ Ⓒ Ⓓ

Unit 12: 説明文問題／読解問題

2. [PART 7] 読解問題

Points

3つの文書
E-mail 1: トピックは、ヨーロッパのパッケージツアー。誰が誰に何の目的で出したのか？
Website: パッケージ ツアーが載っているサイト。対象やコースは？ E-mail 2: 1番目のメールに
対する返事。
1. Karen と Sarah の関係は？　2. Website に記述されていないものは？　3. 2番目の E-mail の
第1段落にキーがある。4. 1番目の E-mail の最後の方にキーがある。5. Website の後半に記述
されていることと、2番目の E-mail の後半に記述されていることを合わせて考慮する。

次の2通の E-mail と Website を読んで、1.~5. の答えとして最も適切なものを (A)~(D) より
選び、その記号をマークしなさい。

To:	Sarah Atwood
From:	Kristen Lopez
Date:	July 24
Subject:	East Europe Travel Package

Sarah,

I've just learned of a package tour in Europe that seems to match well
with your travel goals and budget. One of the tours sponsored by our
sister company has had a couple drop out and they are eager to fill the
spots. The iron is hot!

The package portion of the tour covers Budapest, Vienna and Prague,
but does not include Munich as I know you wanted. Visiting there would
have to be on your own, outside the package.

I've attached a link to the webpage with the tour itinerary. The price is
$5,000, but you'll have to act fast before someone else jumps in.

Look it over and let me know! Say hi to Chet!

Kristen
Pleasant Journeys Travel

71

https://www.graywolftours.com/2025classiceasterneurope_autumn

| Home | Events | Blogs | Membership |

Gray Wolf Tours,
the World's Senior Citizen Travel Leader, presents:

Our 2025 Classic Eastern Europe Autumn Tour Bonanza!

Three Great Cities! Budapest, Vienna and Prague!
Three days in each exciting location!
Enjoy the heart of Fairy Tale Europe!

Tour includes airfare from New York City and back, as well as:

- ALL hotels, ALL overland travel, English-speaking guides throughout, plus all breakfasts and some evening meals too.
- Overland travel is by luxury bus, with some walking required in cities.
- Only $5,000 dollars per traveler for the complete package.
- Click on the link above to view travel dates and the full itinerary.

Unit 12: 説明文問題／読解問題

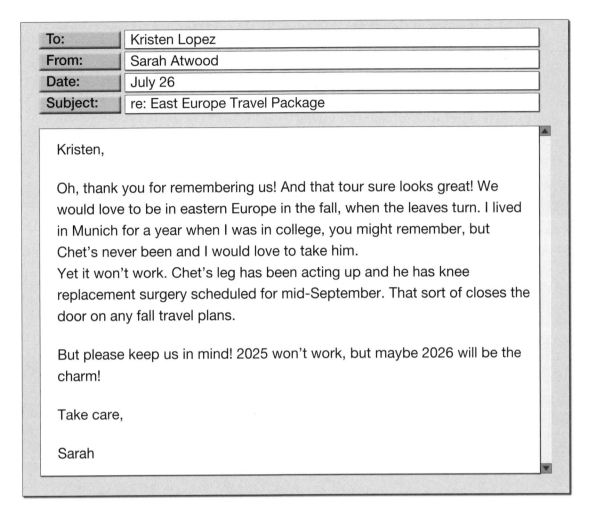

To:	Kristen Lopez
From:	Sarah Atwood
Date:	July 26
Subject:	re: East Europe Travel Package

Kristen,

Oh, thank you for remembering us! And that tour sure looks great! We would love to be in eastern Europe in the fall, when the leaves turn. I lived in Munich for a year when I was in college, you might remember, but Chet's never been and I would love to take him.
Yet it won't work. Chet's leg has been acting up and he has knee replacement surgery scheduled for mid-September. That sort of closes the door on any fall travel plans.

But please keep us in mind! 2025 won't work, but maybe 2026 will be the charm!

Take care,

Sarah

1. What do the two e-mails suggest about Karen's relationship with Sarah?

    (A) They are old friends from college.
    (B) They have consulted on such tours in the past.
    (C) Karen knows Sarah but has never met Chet.
    (D) Sarah and Kristen correspond often.

2. The travel website seems to have several expectations of its travelers. Which of the below is NOT one such expectation?

    (A) Travelers should reach New York City on their own.
    (B) Travelers will be English speakers.
    (C) Travelers must purchase some meals on their own.
    (D) Travelers should be couples.

3. What is true about Sarah Atwood?

  (A) She has been to Europe before.

  (B) She has never met Kristen Lopez.

  (C) She hopes for a cheaper tour.

  (D) She is not fond of autumn travel.

  Ⓐ   Ⓑ   Ⓒ   Ⓓ

4. Why does Kristen urge Sarah to hurry?

  (A) The tour price may go up.

  (B) The tour might leave without them.

  (C) The open spots might not last.

  (D) The tour company is making an exception just for her.

  Ⓐ   Ⓑ   Ⓒ   Ⓓ

5. What in the website content made Sarah hesitant about joining the tour?

  (A) The price seems extravagant.

  (B) The required walking might be hard on Chet.

  (C) Munich is not included in the three main cities.

  (D) She is not an English speaker.

  Ⓐ   Ⓑ   Ⓒ   Ⓓ

	Listening Section			Reading Section		
Part 1	Part 2	Part 3	**Part 4**	Part 5	Part 6	**Part 7**

Unit 13 説明文問題／読解問題

Warm-Up

次の 1. ～ 10. の英文について、------- に入れるべき最も適当なものを (A), (B) より選びなさい。
(カッコ内はこの Unit 中の関連パートを表します。〈例〉Pt3 = Part 3)

1. We need to order additional office ------- such as paper, pens, and toner cartridges. (Pt4)
   (A) issues
   (B) supplies

2. I should ------- with our supplier to confirm the delivery date. (Pt4)
   (A) get acquainted
   (B) get in touch

3. Mike left the office ------- finishing his report due to an emergency. (Pt7)
   (A) prior to
   (B) next to

4. That's just ------- makes this restaurant special — the location and the dishes. (Pt7)
   (A) that
   (B) what

5. Infectious ------- often occur after major floods. (Pt7)
   (A) diseases
   (B) materials

6. Mary and Jane ------- their vacation as the best trip they had ever taken. (Pt7)
   (A) described
   (B) disregarded

7. All meeting participants are required to ------- the quarterly financial report in advance. (Pt7)
   (A) review
   (B) overlook

8. I might get scolded by my boss for ------- the project submission deadline. (Pt7)
   (A) meeting
   (B) missing

75

9. The company will ------- the job opening on their website next Monday. (Pt7)
   (A) remove (B) post

10. Professor Jefferson has given me a new ------- to complete by the end of the week. (Pt7)
    (A) assignment (B) assign

1. [PART 4] 説明文問題

Points

質問文の先読みから、聞き取りのポイントをピックアップ
Questions 1 through 3: 留守電の趣旨は？ Kevin が Kim にしたお礼のわけは？ 注文した数量と届いた数量が異なっていたのはどの商品？

1つの説明文が聞こえてきます。その説明文と注文票に関する1.～3.の質問文の答えとして最も適切なものを (A)～(D) より選び、その記号をマークしなさい。

Order Form #29483 Customer: New Frontiers		
Order Sheet No. 2343B		
Item	Quantity	Price per item
Ballpoint pens	300	$0.99
Staplers	60	$5.99
Erasers	70	$1.25
Notebooks	200	$1.80

1. What is the main reason Kevin Jacobs left a message?
   (A) His company has received too many items.
   (B) He wants to place a different order.
   (C) The order form was no correct.
   (D) Kim Davis forgot to get in touch with him.

   Ⓐ Ⓑ Ⓒ Ⓓ

76

Unit 13: 説明文問題／読解問題

2. Why does Kevin Jacobs express appreciation to Kim Davis?

(A) He does not have to return any of the items.

(B) The office supplies were mailed by Friday.

(C) The products have arrived in good condition.

(D) He has received extra staplers free of charge.

Ⓐ   Ⓑ   Ⓒ   Ⓓ

3. Look at the graphic. Which quantity on the order form does NOT match the number of items sent?

(A) 60

(B) 70

(C) 200

(D) 300

Ⓐ   Ⓑ   Ⓒ   Ⓓ

2. [PART 7] 読解問題

Points

3つの文書
Excerpt: Twobears の著作から抜粋。Student paper: Steve のレポートの一部。E-mail: Brown 教授から Steve へ宛てたメール。
1. バッファローとアメリカ先住民の文化との関係。2. 2つ目の文書から判断。3. 3つ目の文書から判断。4. NG センテンスは？5. Brown 教授の日頃の指導。

次の Excerpt, Student paper と E-mail を読んで、1.~5. の質問の答えとして最も適切なものをそれぞれ (A)~(D) の中より選び、その記号をマークしなさい。

Twobears, Sandra. "Native Americans: History and Traditions." Chicago: Mason Cole, Inc., 2008. Print.

Excerpt from page 102:

Yet the greatest blow to the Indians of the Great Plains was the mass slaughter of the American Bison – the buffalo. While historical animal populations are difficult if not impossible to calculate, fossil and anecdotal evidence point to vast numbers of buffalo prior to the coming of the White man. Some scholars estimate as many as

77

100 million buffalo may have roamed the prairies in the 1600s. Early frontiersmen reported enormous herds, enough to blacken the horizon. As settlers and the railroad pushed west, White hunters used repeating rifles to kill buffalo for their hides and often their tongues, to be served as a delicacy in East Coast restaurants. By the late 1800s a population that was once in the millions had been reduced to less than a thousand. To destroy the buffalo was to destroy Native American culture; and that's just what the White man did!

Steve Johnson
16J21250
19th Century American History
Dr. Brown
May 20

Native Americans of the Great Plains

Excerpt from page three:

More than disease, what really hurt the Indians was the loss of the buffalo. Some scholars say that as many as 100 million buffalo may have roamed the prairies before the White man came. The first frontiersmen described the land as being black with buffalo. White hunters killed buffalo for their hides and tongues, which were then served in East Coast restaurants. By the late 1800s, only a thousand buffalos were left alive. To destroy the buffalo was to destroy Native American culture; and that's just what the White man did!

78

Unit 13: 説明文問題／読解問題

To:	Steve Johnson
From:	Dr. Timothy Brown
Subject:	Your research paper
Date:	May 27

Steve,

I have just reviewed your research paper and I have several criticisms, one severe.

1. You missed the deadline by a full day. The date was clearly printed on the handout I distributed in April and was posted on the class website as well.
2. The assignment called for a minimum of five research sources and you list only four.
3. One paragraph on page three is clearly plagiarized from a book entitled, "Native Americans: History and Culture," by Sandra Twobears, a source you do not list nor cite, with one line taken word for word!

You know what plagiarism is and how seriously I treat it. Your mark on this paper and your class credit are in jeopardy. I wish to speak to you about this in person. My office hours are from 1:00 to 5:00 on Wednesday. I expect to see you then.

Tim Brown

1. According to the excerpt, what is most likely true about the buffalo?
   (A) Buffalo were a staple food for white hunters.
   (B) Buffalo numbers were cut in half over 200 years.
   (C) As settlers pushed west, buffalo moved east.
   (D) As buffalo numbers declined, Native American cultures were destroyed.

79

2. From Steve's paper, what might we assume to be another problem suffered by Native Americans, other than the loss of buffalo?
   (A) White hunters
   (B) Illness of some kind
   (C) Frontiersmen
   (D) The eating habits of easterners

3. What seems to be the main reason that Steve may fail the class?
   (A) He submitted his paper after the posted deadline.
   (B) He had too many resources.
   (C) He did not follow directions properly.
   (D) He copied another writer without giving credit.

4. Which of these sentences from Steve's paper would appear to upset Dr. Brown the most?
   (A) White hunters killed buffalo for their hides and tongues, which were then served in east coast restaurants.
   (B) To destroy the buffalo was to destroy Native American culture; and that's just what the White man did!
   (C) Some scholars say that as many as 100 million buffalo may have roamed the prairies before the White man came.
   (D) More than disease and battles with soldiers, what really hurt the Indians was the loss of the buffalo.

5. Which of the following can we assume about Dr. Brown and his class?
   (A) He has lectured on Native Americans and American Bison.
   (B) He uses the Sandra Twobears book as a text.
   (C) He has taught students not to copy others' work without acknowledgement.
   (D) He is not strict about rules.

TOEIC® L&R
Review Test 1

（Listening 50 問 +Reading 50 問）

※解答用紙は巻末に収録しています。

Review Test 1

LISTENING SECTION

PART 1　[写真描写問題]

次の 1.～3. の写真について、それぞれの写真を説明する英文が 4 つ聞こえてきます。最も適切な英文を (A) ～ (D) より選び、その記号を解答用紙にマークしなさい。

 1.

 2.

Review Test 1

 3.

PART 2　[応答問題]

英文が聞こえ、その英文につづいて (A)(B)(C) 3つの応答文が聞こえます。4.~17. の英文に対する最も適切な応答文を (A)~(C) より選び、その記号を解答用紙にマークしなさい。

 4. Mark your answer on your sheet.

5. Mark your answer on your sheet.

6. Mark your answer on your sheet.

 7. Mark your answer on your sheet.

8. Mark your answer on your sheet.

9. Mark your answer on your sheet.

83

10. Mark your answer on your sheet.

11. Mark your answer on your sheet.

12. Mark your answer on your sheet.

 13. Mark your answer on your sheet.

14. Mark your answer on your sheet.

15. Mark your answer on your sheet.

 16. Mark your answer on your sheet.

17. Mark your answer on your sheet.

PART 3 ［会話問題］

6つの会話を聞き、それぞれの会話に関する18.～35.の質問文の答えとして最も適切なものを(A)～(D) より選び、その記号を解答用紙にマークしなさい。

 18. What are the man and woman talking about?
- (A) A group of language students
- (B) A group of Spanish tourists
- (C) A group of Italian doctors
- (D) A group of Brazilian businesspeople

19. What language were the visitors speaking when Charlie saw them?
- (A) Spanish
- (B) English
- (C) Italian
- (D) Portuguese

20. What does Jeanne suggest to Charlie?
- (A) Working late at the office
- (B) Taking the visitors out
- (C) Eating with the Brazilians
- (D) Seeing quality control

Review Test 1

 21. What is the woman complaining about?
   (A) She has to fix breakfast for her children in the morning.
   (B) She feels her co-worker arrives too early.
   (C) Her ride to work is uncomfortable.
   (D) She is so busy in the morning.

22. Why does the man prefer the local train?
   (A) He doesn't have to stand.
   (B) He enjoys the longer ride.
   (C) He is an early riser.
   (D) He doesn't need to make breakfast for his family.

23. What does the man suggest that the woman do?
   (A) Get up early and take the local train.
   (B) Put her children first.
   (C) Avoid crowded trains.
   (D) Be patient until her kids get older.

 24. What is the man inviting the woman to do?
   (A) Go to a meeting with the new employee.
   (B) Join him for lunch at a French restaurant.
   (C) Eat her sandwich for dinner.
   (D) Buy a more expensive sandwich.

25. Why did Mary seem a bit upset at Steve?
   (A) He did not invite Lisa to the lunch.
   (B) He did not inform her sooner.
   (C) He chose a restaurant that is expensive.
   (D) He was not going to pay for the lunch.

26. Why is Mary going for lunch with Steve?
   (A) She can eat at the restaurant for dinner.
   (B) She hasn't had French cuisine for a long time.
   (C) She found out that the lunch is free.
   (D) She wants to talk to a new employee.

27. What is the woman worried about?
(A) Mr. Johnson is not sending the drawings at all.
(B) She has not received the design details.
(C) The meeting is rescheduled to an earlier time.
(D) The head office is too far to reach on time.

28. What industry does Mr. Johnson most likely work in?
(A) Delivery
(B) Manufacturing
(C) Design
(D) Telecommunications

29. When should the final design be ready?
(A) By 6:00 P.M.
(B) By the next day's morning
(C) By the meeting the next day
(D) By the time of release

30. What the does man imply when he says "... it wasn't a motivating factor?"
(A) His branch was not motivated to sell more units.
(B) The increase in sales was not related to potential layoffs.
(C) The sales spike had no effect on his clients.
(D) His branch needs to work harder.

31. What seems to be the relationship between the two speakers?
(A) The woman is higher in the company than the man.
(B) The man is higher in the company than the woman.
(C) The woman is one of the man's employees.
(D) The man is one of the woman's clients.

32. Why does the man feel confident for the current quarter?
(A) His branch may sell 600 units this time.
(B) He has paid some clients off.
(C) His branch is currently selling more than last quarter.
(D) He is no longer fearful of layoffs.

Review Test 1

 33. What does the man hope to do?

  (A) Arrive at the airport early
  (B) Buy a new ticket to Chicago
  (C) Take an earlier flight to Chicago
  (D) Change his flight to a different city

34. Why is there a 100-dollar fee?

  (A) The man's ticket does not allow for any changes.
  (B) Reservations can never be changed free of charge.
  (C) Seats are not available on the flight to Chicago.
  (D) The man did not change his reservation soon enough.

35. What does the man mean when he says, "I was under a different impression"?

  (A) His understanding is not the same as the woman's.
  (B) He disagrees with the airline's flight plan.
  (C) His ticket cannot be changed free of charge.
  (D) He refuses to pay the 100-dollar fee.

PART 4 　[説明文問題]

説明文が5つ聞こえてきます。それぞれの説明文に関する36.～50.の質問の答えとして最も適切なものを (A)～(D) より選び、その記号を解答用紙にマークしなさい。

 36. Why was the location of the stockholder's meeting changed?

  (A) The company has a new headquarters building.
  (B) The company can ensure adequate seating for everyone.
  (C) There were some security problems previously.
  (D) The meetings can be held in a room with a view.

37. Which item of business will be discussed first?

  (A) The election of new officers
  (B) The location of the next meeting
  (C) The ideas and concerns of the stockholders
  (D) The security issues

87

38. Which people should fill out the blue cards?
  (A) The stockholders who want to vote
  (B) The stockholders who cannot attend the meeting
  (C) The candidates for president
  (D) The people concerned about security

---

39. Why is this store extending its shopping time?
  (A) It plans to close later in the month.
  (B) It wishes to accommodate holiday season shoppers.
  (C) Regular hours are more than enough.
  (D) It wishes to reach shoppers living more than twenty miles away.

40. What time will the store close on Dec. 27th?
  (A) At ten p.m.
  (B) At six p.m.
  (C) At twelve noon.
  (D) The store will not open that day.

41. What is an extra advantage for shoppers living near the store?
  (A) They can receive free delivery.
  (B) They can receive extended shopping.
  (C) They can use Highway 17.
  (D) They can shop during the holiday season.

---

42. Where can you get fresh investing ideas?
  (A) At Fat City
  (B) At Profit City
  (C) At Main Street City
  (D) At Breakout City

43. When does Stock Search become available?
  (A) Daily   (B) Weekly   (C) Bimonthly   (D) Monthly

Review Test 1

44. What can you choose from?
    (A) A dozen stock predictions
    (B) Surging volume
    (C) Explosive growth rates
    (D) Insider buying

45. What seems to be the problem with the new web site?
    (A) The IT Office is too busy.
    (B) Too many people are complaining.
    (C) Users have to keep logging on.
    (D) It's under the control of the IT office.

46. Why is the man unable to do anything about the log-on situation?
    (A) He has had the same difficulty himself.
    (B) The problem is not under his control.
    (C) He's heard the same complaint from everyone.
    (D) The IT office has a better suggestion.

47. What does the man encourage everyone do?
    (A) To complain to the IT office directly.
    (B) To keep logging on.
    (C) To adjourn the meeting.
    (D) To change their log-on methods.

48. Who is the intended audience for this speech?
    (A) Employees of this company
    (B) Friends of the chairperson
    (C) New owners of the business
    (D) Magazine writers

49. What is Ms. Bixby's current position?
    (A) President   (B) Manager   (C) Chair   (D) Clerk

50. What happened when the owners changed?
    (A) A new president was hired.
    (B) Many employees left the company.
    (C) The president stayed the same.
    (D) The profits started to go down.

89

READING SECTION

PART 5 [短文穴埋め問題]

次の 51.～65. の英文について、------- に入れるべき最も適当なものをそれぞれ (A) ～ (D) より
選び、その記号を解答用紙にマークしなさい。

51. The new TV commercial proved highly -------, increasing sales by 20% in
just three months.
(A) possessive   (B) disappointed   (C) effective   (D) successive

52. The excitement shown by the ------- at the concert was less than we had
expected.
(A) popularity   (B) audience   (C) evacuation   (D) feature

53. Our manager would like to ------- his gratitude to all the employees in the
sales department.
(A) talk   (B) inform   (C) convey   (D) instruct

54. ------- customer satisfaction, we have also experienced a significant increase in sales growth.
(A) Ahead of   (B) Instead of   (C) Apart from   (D) Far from

55. Our Customer's Service Department serves notice that goods or merchan-
dise at this store may not be -------.
(A) excused   (B) exchanged   (C) excluded   (D) excepted

56. Labor and Management will hold a meeting to ------- their opinions.
(A) dictate   (B) disapprove   (C) discuss   (D) discourse

57. Mr. Lee's report had ------- typos, making it very easy to read.
(A) certain   (B) all   (C) each   (D) few

58. If the employees work -------, the project will never be completed on time.
(A) any slower   (B) more slower   (C) some slower   (D) most slowest

59. Mr. Johnson will never amount to much in this company simply because
he is -------.
(A) impossible   (B) incapable   (C) possible   (D) convenient

90

Review Test 1

60. This antique vase ------- the ones found in ancient Roman ruins.

(A) appears   (B) terminates   (C) resembles   (D) overlooks

61. As long as Cambell's Industries doesn't give -------, the dairy production lines will be maintained.

(A) over   (B) out   (C) up   (D) off

62. To get to the other side, it is necessary to walk ------- the street.

(A) across   (B) along   (C) away   (D) aside

63. The company decided to reinvest its ------- profits in developing new products.

(A) surplus   (B) rate   (C) margin   (D) completion

64. My boss didn't know about the merger, and I didn't -------.

(A) either   (B) neither   (C) too   (D) also

65. Due to the -------, the economic forecast doesn't look as good as we had expected.

(A) growth   (B) recession   (C) production   (D) upturn

PART 6 [長文穴埋め問題]

次の２つの英文中の 66.～73. の空所に入れるべき最も適切なものを、それぞれ (A)～(D) より選び、その記号を解答用紙にマークしなさい。

The city of Green Lake would like to congratulate Setsuko Summers on reaching 100 years of age. Setsuko is not only our community's --------- living
66.
citizen — she is also the oldest person ever to live in Green Lake. Setsuko, who --------- from Yokohama, Japan, came to Green Lake in 1954 with her
67.
husband Doug, who passed away last year. --------- But later she became a
68.
Japanese teacher and started the first Japanese language program in the state at Green Lake High School in 1959. The program became the model for future Japanese language programs throughout the state. Setsuko --------- in 1999 at
69.
the age of 75, but today she still teaches one class a week at the high school.

66. (A) most individual   (B) least serious
    (C) oldest   (D) youngest

67. (A) come   (B) comes   (C) came   (D) coming

68. (A) Setsuko was the first Japanese teacher in the Green Lake.
    (B) Setsuko couldn't speak English well when she first arrived in the US.
    (C) Setsuko has missed her husband ever since.
    (D) Setsuko changed her career and life.

69. (A) is retiring   (B) has retired
    (C) will be retiring   (D) retired

Review Test 1

Dear Sir or Madam:

I am writing to recommend Tim Putnam for the position of international accounts manager at L&L Trading. As Tim's graduate school professor, I can attest to his dedication. He ---------- his thesis in international trading for the past year,
70.
interviewing executives at trading companies and compiling data sheets to support his arguments.

With the completion of his thesis this month, Tim will be receiving a Master's degree in International Trade and Commerce, ---------- to be awarded. Tim will
71.
be among the few who will have the unique opportunity to shape the global business market of the future.

---------- This past year he has been my personal assistant, teaching and
72.
counseling undergraduates and grading their papers. At the same time, he has ---------- in his studies, working hard to stay at the top of his class. What's more,
73.
he is very sociable with his classmates and has the communications skills that are essential to do business.
I recommend Tim Putnam very highly for this position.
Sincerely,
Martha Peters, Ph.D.

70. (A) is working on
    (C) worked on
    (B) had worked on
    (D) has been working on

71. (A) the kind of its first
    (C) the first kind of its
    (B) its the first kind of
    (D) the first of its kind

72. (A) It was a compelling experience for Tim.
    (B) Tim was supposed to graduate this year.
    (C) Tim showed improper practices.
    (D) Tim is a highly capable person.

73. (A) persisted   (B) engrossed   (C) immersed   (D) involved

93

PART 7　[読解問題]

次の Coupon を読んで、74.~75. の質問の答えとして最も適切なものをそれぞれ (A)~(D) より
選び、その記号を解答用紙にマークしなさい。

Sava Grill Discount Coupon

Enjoy a delicious meal with great savings!

REGULAR PRICE / DISCOUNT PRICE

ADULTS (ages 13–60) $30.00 / **$25.00**

CHILDREN (ages 7–12) $20.00 / **$15.00**

Special Note: Infants (ages 0-6) eat for free!

Terms and Conditions:
- This coupon can be used for up to 4 people.
- Valid on weekdays only.
- Cannot be combined with other offers.
- Expires: December 31, 202

---

74. How much would a family of two adults and two children save using this coupon?

(A) $10　　　　(B) $20　　　　(C) $30　　　　(D) $40

75. What is most likely true about the coupon?

(A) The coupon can be used multiple times.
(B) The coupon is valid for a limited time only.
(C) The coupon is applicable to all items in the store.
(D) The coupon requires a minimum purchase amount.

Review Test 1

次の Notice を読んで、76.～77. の質問の答えとして最も適切なものをそれぞれ (A)～(D) より選び、その記号を解答用紙にマークしなさい。

IMPORTANT NOTICE

We wish to draw your attention to the benefits of joining the company health insurance scheme (see attachment). This insurance provides members and their families with excellent protection. Since a major portion of the cost is covered by the company, the price to members is very reasonable and we feel you should give it your most serious consideration .

All staff who have not yet enrolled in the health scheme should notice that there is an opportunity for them to do so during the coming month. Employees who are already enrolled may make changes to their policies during this period if they so desire.

Yours sincerely,

A. T. Bottomley
Arnold T. Bottomley
Human Resources

---

76. Who probably wrote this notice?
    (A) The board of directors
    (B) An insurance agent
    (C) The personnel department
    (D) A cost accountant

77. What kind of employees might choose to ignore this notification?
    (A) Those not covered by a health scheme
    (B) Those unhappy with their existing health scheme
    (C) Those already covered by a spouse's health scheme
    (D) Those who wish to change their insurance coverage

次の Memo を読んで、78.～79. の質問の答えとして最も適切なものをそれぞれ (A)～(D) より
選び、その記号を解答用紙にマークしなさい。

MEMO

From: Sarah Johnson, HR Manager
To: All Employees
Date: September 27
Re: New Remote Work Policy

Starting next month, we will be implementing a new remote work policy to
provide more flexibility for our employees. This policy will allow eligible
employees to work from home up to three days a week. The goal is to
improve work-life balance and increase productivity.

Key points of the new policy include:

Eligibility: Employees who have been with the company for at least six
months.
Equipment: The company will provide necessary equipment such as
laptops and headsets.
Communication: Regular check-ins with managers are required to ensure
smooth workflow.
Security: Employees must follow all company security protocols while
working remotely.
We will hold a virtual meeting on October 5 to discuss the details and
answer any questions you may have. Please mark your calendars and look
out for the meeting invite.

---

78. What is the main purpose of the memo?

    (A) To announce a new project

    (B) To introduce a new employee

    (C) To inform about a new remote work policy

    (D) To schedule a team-building event

79. What is NOT mentioned as part of the new remote work policy?

(A) Eligibility criteria
(B) Equipment provision
(C) Salary increase
(D) Security protocols

次の Text-message chain を読んで、80.~81. の質問の答えとして最も適切なものをそれぞれ (A)~(D) より選び、その記号を解答用紙にマークしなさい。

80. What can we assume is Mary's purpose in sending John the attachment?

(A) John is her boss and she needs his approval.
(B) She is John's boss and she is informing him about the meeting.
(C) She wishes John to check the content of her file.
(D) She is new and not yet accustomed to her job.

81. At 8:21 P.M., what does Mary mean when she writes, "Oops!"?

(A) She is expressing thanks that John caught her error.

(B) She is showing irritation with her errant spelling.

(C) She is voicing embarrassment over her mistake.

(D) She is asking John's forgiveness for her error.

次の Web site を読んで、82.~84. の質問の答えとして最も適切なものを、それぞれ (A)~(D) の中より選び、その記号を解答用紙にマークしなさい。

Home	Events	Blogs	Membership

https://www.aussiesoverseas.com

Aussies Overseas is your one-stop online shopping spot for foods and gift items from Australia. If you miss your home Down Under and yearn to taste Australian treats not available in your local stores, you have come to the right place!

Aussie Overseas offers over five hundred items produced only in Australia, ranging all the way from kangaroo steaks to didgeridoos. We will ship to any address we can feasibly reach. And if what you want isn't listed on our web site, drop us a line and we'll do our best to make your Australian dreams come true. Aussies Overseas takes pride in its satisfied customers!

82. What kind of items does this web site sell?

(A) Items that cannot be shipped overseas

(B) Items that all Australian people miss

(C) Items made and sold in Australia

(D) Items available in local stores

83. What should web site visitors do if they can't find an item they wish?

(A) They should try a local store.

(B) They should shop on this web site.

(C) They should send the web site a request.

(D) They should move to a feasible address.

98

84. To whom does this web site mainly market its goods?

(A) People living Down Under

(B) Australians residing abroad

(C) Foreigners who are interested in Australia

(D) Unsatisfied Australian shoppers

次の E-mail を読んで、85.~87. の質問の答えとして最も適切なものをそれぞれ (A)~(D) より選び、その記号を解答用紙にマークしなさい。

To:	Linda Moore <lmoore@irismail.com>
From:	Brian Miller <bmiller@techgenius.com>
Date:	25 September
Subject:	Apology for Shipping Delay of Your PhantomXL Smartwatch

Dear Ms. Moore,

We hope this message finds you well. We regret to inform you that the shipment of your PhantomXL Smartwatch has been delayed due to unforeseen logistical issues. We understand the inconvenience this may cause and sincerely apologize for the delay.

Your order is now expected to arrive by October 5. We kindly ask for your patience and understanding as we work to ensure your product reaches you as soon as possible. If you wish to cancel your order, please contact us by October 1st.

If you have any questions or need further assistance, please do not hesitate to contact us.

Thank you for your understanding and continued support.

Best regards,

Brian Miller
Customer Service Team
TechGenius Inc.

85. What is a purpose of the e-mail?

    (A) To confirm the shipping date

    (B) To apologize for the delay in shipping

    (C) To offer a discount on future purchases.

    (D) To inform of road congestion.

86. Why is the shipment delayed?

    (A) The product is out of stock.

    (B) There was an issue with the payment.

    (C) The delivery company is facing unexpected delays.

    (D) The customer provided an incorrect address.

87. What most likely would make Ms. Moore cancel this order?

    (A) She found a better price elsewhere.

    (B) She feels that the product's arrival date is too late.

    (C) She no longer needs the product.

    (D) She is unhappy with the customer service.

次の News article / Obituary を読んで、88.～90. の質問の答えとして最も適切なものを、それぞれ (A)～(D) の中より選び、その記号を解答用紙にマークしなさい。

Longtime Mayville resident Daniel Carpenter passed away on Tuesday morning, August 6th, at County Hospital, following a brief illness. He was 78.

Daniel was born in Mayville in 1946, the son of Issac and Jean Carpenter. He graduated from Mayville High School in 1963, served in the United States Navy until 1968, and was then employed by the city as a fireman until his retirement in 2011. He married Victoria Gallagher in 1973 and she survives, as does their son James, his wife Ann, and two grandchildren, Kathy and Bennet. He was preceded in death by his parents and an older brother, Robert.

Daniel was an avid fisherman. He fished at Sun Lake Park almost every morning and was well-known to all lake visitors. He will be mourned by his family and many friends, including those in the City Fire Department.

Funeral arrangements are currently pending at Riverview Funeral Home in Mayville.

Review Test 1

88. What was Daniel Carpenter's cause of death?

(A) He had a brief illness.

(B) He passed away at the hospital.

(C) It is currently pending at a funeral home.

(D) The exact cause is not stated.

89. What did Daniel do upon graduation from high school?

(A) He passed away.

(B) He worked in the fire department.

(C) He joined the Navy.

(D) He married Victoria Gallagher.

90. The word "avid" in paragraph 3, line 1, is closest in meaning to

(A) vivid   (B) active

(C) indifferent   (D) renowned

次の Book review を読んで、91.～93. の質問の答えとして最も適切なものを、それぞれ (A)～(D) の中より選び、その記号を解答用紙にマークしなさい。

"The Evolution of Technology: From Stone Tools to Smart Devices" is a captivating journey through the history of human innovation. Written by Dr. Emily Thompson, a renowned historian and technologist, this book meticulously traces the development of technology from the earliest stone tools to the latest smart devices. Dr. Thompson's extensive research and engaging writing style make complex technological advancements accessible and fascinating. She brings historical figures to life with vivid anecdotes and explores how each technological leap has shaped human society. Even readers who are not typically interested in technology will find themselves engrossed in this well-crafted narrative.

91. What is the primary focus of this book review?

(A) The history of human societies

(B) The development of technology

(C) The evolution of biological species

(D) The history of art and culture

92. What makes Dr. Thompson's writing style engaging according to the review?

    (A) Her use of technical jargon

    (B) Her vivid anecdotes and accessible explanations

    (C) Her focus on financial news

    (D) Her detailed descriptions of ancient artifacts

93. What is NOT indicated in this book review?

    (A) The book's main theme and central message.

    (B) The impact of technological advancements on human society

    (C) The extensive research by the author.

    (D) The author's previous works and biography.

次の Text-message chain を読んで、94.～96. の質問の答えとして最も適切なものを、それぞれ (A)～(D) の中から選び、その記号を解答用紙にマークしなさい。

Jackie (7:22 P.M.)
What are you guys getting Diane for her birthday? We don't want to buy the same things. I'm giving her some eyeliner, since she always borrows mine. Maybe an eyeliner kit.

Megan (8:01 P.M.)
LOL! She borrows my eyeliner too! I think I'll get her a phone charger for the same reason. She borrows mine almost every day.

Jackie (8:05 P.M.)
Right. She borrows mine sometimes too.

Shelia (8:33 P.M.)
She and I have this exchange we've been doing since high school. I always buy her a teddy bear and then on my birthday, she does the same for me.

Megan (8:41 P.M.)
How cute!

Jackie (8:43 P.M.)
My birthday's next month. Get me one too!

Karen (9:04 P.M.)
A teddy bear! Oh no! Guess what I bought!

Shelia (9:12 P.M.)
I wouldn't worry about it. We all know how Diane loves teddy bears.

Jackie (9:19 P.M.)
Give it to me! LOL!

---

94. What is Jackie worried about?

(A) She wants to ensure everyone chooses a different gift.

(B) She wants to stop Diane from borrowing her things.

(C) She hopes to receive a teddy bear.

(D) She is thinking about her birthday next month.

95. Who will receive the teddy bear that Karen bought?

(A) Jackie   (B) Megan   (C) Diane   (D) Karen

96. Which of the participants seems to have known Diane the longest?

(A) Jackie   (B) Megan   (C) Shelia   (D) Karen

次の Job listing を読んで、97.~100. の質問の答えとして最も適切なものを、それぞれ (A)~(D) の中より選び、その記号を解答用紙にマークしなさい。

Job Opening at Tech Innovators Inc.

Position: Software Developer

Anticipated Start Date: 1 November

Location: Tech Innovators Headquarters, 5th Floor, Development Wing

Reports to: Lead Software Engineer

Major Duties:

1. Develop and maintain web applications using modern frameworks.
2. Collaborate with cross-functional teams to define and design new features.
3. Ensure the performance, quality, and responsiveness of applications.
4. Identify and correct bottlenecks and fix bugs.

Application review begins 15 October.

To apply: Send resume and cover letter to Randy Taylor, manager of human resources, at rtaylor@techinnovators.com.

103

97. What is NOT listed in the job listing?

(A) The name of the employer

(B) The date that the application review begins

(C) The name of the Lead Software Engineer

(D) The date that the job starts

98. What does the listing indicate about Tech Innovators?

(A) The head office is on the top floor.

(B) The head office will be completed soon.

(C) There will be training before you start work.

(D) There are multiple job duties.

99. What are the job requirements?

(A) Long experience in web application development

(B) Ability to communicate well with other departments

(C) Reporting to a lead software engineer on a daily basis

(D) A wide range of practical skills for web application development

100. What will happen on October 15?

(A) The HR department begins the selection process.

(B) The HR department conducts interviews.

(C) Selected candidates go to the HR department.

(D) Applications are closed.

TOEIC® L&R
Review Test 2

（Listening 50 問 +Reading 50 問）

※解答用紙は巻末に収録しています。

Review Test 2

LISTENING SECTION

PART 1　[写真描写問題]

次の 1.~3. の写真について、それぞれの写真を説明する英文が 4 つ聞こえてきます。最も適切な英文を (A)~(D) より選び、その記号を解答用紙にマークしなさい。

 1.

 2.

Review Test 2

 3.

PART 2 ［応答問題］

英文が聞こえ、その英文につづいて (A)(B)(C) 3つの応答文が聞こえます。4.〜17.の英文に対する最も適切な応答文を (A)〜(C) より選び、その記号を解答用紙にマークしなさい。

 4. Mark your answer on your sheet.

5. Mark your answer on your sheet.

6. Mark your answer on your sheet.

 7. Mark your answer on your sheet.

8. Mark your answer on your sheet.

9. Mark your answer on your sheet.

 10. Mark your answer on your sheet.

107

11. Mark your answer on your sheet.

12. Mark your answer on your sheet.

 13. Mark your answer on your sheet.

14. Mark your answer on your sheet.

15. Mark your answer on your sheet.

 16. Mark your answer on your sheet.

17. Mark your answer on your sheet.

PART 3 [会話問題]

6つの会話を聞き、それぞれの会話に関する 18.~35. の質問文の答えとして最も適切なものを (A) ~ (D) より選び、その記号を解答用紙にマークしなさい。

 18. What are the man and woman talking about?
- (A) A hotel reservation
- (B) Sweet dreams
- (C) The ABC Company
- (D) Quitting smoking

19. What is the man most likely doing?
- (A) He's on vacation.
- (B) He's on a business trip.
- (C) He's leaving a hotel.
- (D) He's going home.

20. What will the woman do?
- (A) Wake Mr. Jones next morning
- (B) Make coffee for Mr. Jones
- (C) Make the man's hotel reservation
- (D) Answer the man's phone calls

Review Test 2

 21. What are the speakers mainly discussing?
   (A) The report on health
   (B) Bill's health
   (C) The woman's health
   (D) Bill's new home

22. What does Bill think of the woman's idea?
   (A) He doesn't like it.
   (B) He wants to think about it.
   (C) He believes it's good.
   (D) He thinks it isn't right.

23. What will happen to the report?
   (A) Bill will write it at a later time.
   (B) The others will write it without Bill.
   (C) The woman will call Bill about it.
   (D) They are just about finished with it.

 24. When was one of Jim's umbrellas taken?
   (A) Last month   (B) Last week
   (C) Yesterday   (D) This afternoon

25. Where is this conversation most likely taking place?
   (A) At Hitchens' house   (B) In a station
   (C) In an office   (D) In an elevator

26. Where does Jim think would be a better place for the umbrellas?
   (A) Near the elevator   (B) In Hitchens' office
   (C) Closer to the desks   (D) Inside the company

 27. What is the reason that the woman prefers the bus?
   (A) She has no interest in the historic district.
   (B) She thinks stopping at cafes will be costly.
   (C) She dislikes walking.
   (D) She is feeling fatigued.

109

28. What factor seems to influence the first speaker's decision to walk?
    (A) He wants to satisfy the woman.
    (B) He likes the thought of saving money.
    (C) He is hungry for pastry.
    (D) He wants to see as much as he can.

29. Why does the third speaker suggest that walking is better?
    (A) Walking will lead to nice pastry shops.
    (B) Walking is easier than the bus.
    (C) Walking is quicker than the bus.
    (D) Walking helps see the city in more detail.

30. Why does Jim want Laura to help him?
    (A) He is going to see his client.
    (B) He is busy talking to his boss.
    (C) He is talking to a client now.
    (D) He is writing the report now.

31. What does the woman imply when she says "I won't be able to do it for 30 minutes or so"?
    (A) She was talking on the phone.
    (B) She was busy with her work.
    (C) She had never been to the seventh floor.
    (D) She didn't finish her report yet.

32. Who is probably going to go to the 7th floor?
    (A) Bill   (B) Laura   (C) Mr. Davies   (D) Jim

Review Test 2

June 15th Presentation Schedule

9:00

"Making Better Use of Urban Green Spaces," by Susan P. Lange: Room 223

"Micro-Plastic in our Diets," by Dr. Matthew Oliver: Room 245

10:30

"Recent Developments in Renewable Energy," by Dr. Ellen Ross: Room 212

"Protecting Wildlife in Changing Ecosystems," by Dr. Wilson Pruitt: Room 303

12:00 to 1:30

Lunch in the Johnson Hall cafeteria

1:30

"Deforestation and its Effects," by Dr. Karen E. Smith: Room 245

"Saving our Coral Reefs" by Yuta Omura: Room 313

4:30

"New Water Conservation Technologies," by Victoria Lopez & Ernesto Rivera, Room 212

"Waste Management and the Environment" by Scott Henderson, Room 303

---

 33. What is the woman's problem?

  (A) She misread the schedule.

  (B) She can't find Dr. Oliver's presentation.

  (C) She has arrived too late.

  (D) She doesn't know the correct room number.

34. What does the woman request from the man?

  (A) She wants to meet Dr. Oliver.

  (B) She wants him to return in one hour.

  (C) She asks for the updated schedule.

  (D) She asks for a room change.

35. Look at the graphic. According to the new schedule, whose presentation might conflict with that of Dr. Oliver's?

  (A) Wilson Pruitt's   (B) Dr. Smith's

  (C) Yuta Omura's   (D) No one's

111

PART 4　[説明文問題]

説明文が5つ聞こえてきます。それぞれの説明文に関する36.〜50. の質問の答えとして最も適切なものを (A)〜(D) より選び、その記号を解答用紙にマークしなさい。

36. What benefits will subscribers receive from Jack's videos?
    (A) Conversation with Hollywood stars
    (B) A trip to Hollywood
    (C) Fitness instruction
    (D) Monthly Internet access

37. What does Jack say is the secret to healthy Hollywood performers?
    (A) Looking younger
    (B) Having better muscle tone
    (C) Subscribing to his videos
    (D) Following his fitness routine

38. How often will subscribers receive Jack's videos?
    (A) Every day.　(B) Every week　(C) Every month　(D) Twice a month

39. What kind of event is this?
    (A) Shareholders meeting
    (B) Ongoing department store sale
    (C) Recent department store opening
    (D) Annual company convention

40. How many EcBuy's stores are there in North America?
    (A) 2 percent more than last year
    (B) Over 100 stores
    (C) About 1000 stores altogether
    (D) Around 100 stores

41. According to Bill Munny, what must EcBuy's do now?
    (A) Clean their stores to be more professional
    (B) Become the biggest in all world markets
    (C) Improve service, such as speed and efficiency
    (D) Become the fastest-serving department store

Review Test 2

 42. What is the main purpose of this announcement?
  (A) Explaining construction
  (B) Counting vehicles
  (C) Giving a cost estimate
  (D) Locating road lanes

43. What does 450 refer to?
  (A) The number of cars that can be carried per hour
  (B) The number of kilometers long that the bridge will be
  (C) The length in meters for each span
  (D) The width in meters of the bridge

44. How high will the bridge be?
  (A) Between 65 and 70 meters
  (B) Between 70 and 75 meters
  (C) Between 75 and 80 meters
  (D) Between 80 and 85 meters

 45. What must passengers do with the information forms?
  (A) Present them to the attendant
  (B) Write them in both Japanese and English
  (C) Fill them out before passing through customs
  (D) Use them to transfer to other international destinations

46. What should passengers do if they are not Japanese?
  (A) They should fill out the form as well.
  (B) They should ask the attendant for help.
  (C) They should not pass through customs.
  (D) They should not remain in Japan.

47. Why does the speaker say, "transferring to another international destination"?
  (A) The passengers cannot transfer without the form.
  (B) The passengers have no need for the form.
  (C) The passengers might not follow English or Japanese.
  (D) The passengers need to pass through customs first.

113

Enterprise Publications. Product Order	
Order #	82304
Shipping date	March 10
Billing address	Springfield Board of Education 2345 Parkway Place Springfield, MO. 83950
Shipping address	Central Junior High School 2914 Park Lane Springfield, MO 83857
Shipping method (circle preference)	Regular mail Express overnight

 48. What was Bob's request to Julie?
- (A) To find out where the textbooks were sent
- (B) To send him a different order form
- (C) To choose the shipping preference
- (D) To contact the client for him

49. Why is Bob in a hurry?
- (A) The client wants the books by the end of the day.
- (B) The order has to be sent today.
- (C) The overnight mail will arrive soon.
- (D) The regular service is too slow.

50. Look at the graphic. Where will the textbooks be sent?
- (A) Enterprise Publications
- (B) Springfield Board of Education
- (C) Central Junior High School
- (D) Parkway Place

READING SECTION

PART 5 [短文穴埋め問題]

次の 51.～65. の英文について、------- に入れるべき最も適当なものをそれぞれ (A) ～ (D) より選び、その記号を解答用紙にマークしなさい。

51. This revised insurance policy is so comprehensive that it will ------- for full coverage in case of mishandling.

(A) deliver   (B) furnish   (C) provide   (D) distribute

52. I was just talking to Mr. Smith about the ------- of the money.

(A) disappear   (B) disappears

(C) disappeared   (D) disappearance

53. Mr. Reynolds organized the company party quickly ------- efficiently.

(A) but   (B) and   (C) nor   (D) or

54. Let's ------- the issue at the committee meeting on Friday.

(A) address   (B) speak   (C) chat   (D) say

55. I'll ------- by your office later to discuss the new product development.

(A) go   (B) get   (C) pass   (D) drop

56. As the last customer was ------- an account at the bank, two strange men asked him for his ID.

(A) opening   (B) ordering   (C) offering   (D) occupying

57. The amount that had to be paid was greater than the total of the receipts -------.

(A) united   (B) collected   (C) consisted   (D) implicated

58. The cost of living in the city is ------- higher than in the countryside.

(A) temporarily   (B) additionally   (C) immediately   (D) comparatively

59. The hospital is known for its ------- approach to surgery and patient care

(A) serious   (B) progressive   (C) accidental   (D) occasional

115

60. The clinic sent my grandfather a ------- about his dental appointment next Monday.

(A) ill   (B) memory   (C) reminder   (D) contract

61. It is necessary for Tomco Company and Crenshaw Incorporated to get ------- in order to realize their current profit margin.

(A) along   (B) after   (C) back   (D) away

62. We appreciate your patience ------- we check the product's availability.

(A) except   (B) although   (C) while   (D) if

63. While maintaining ------- exercise routines is important, overdoing it can negatively impact your overall health.

(A) continuously   (B) continuous   (C) continued   (D) continue

64. Mr. Bradley would like to speak to one and ------- so that nobody will be in doubt about the situation we are in.

(A) many   (B) all   (C) each   (D) few

65. The company ------- increased its market share by introducing new products every quarter.

(A) incrementally   (B) approximately

(C) briefly   (D) occasionally

Review Test 2

PART 6 [長文穴埋め問題]

次の 2 つの英文中の 66. ～ 73. の空所に入れるべき最も適切なものを、それぞれ (A) ～ (D) より選び、その記号を解答用紙にマークしなさい。

Jim, sorry to write out of the ---66.---. It's been a while. I hope you and Cathy are both fine. I'm writing because I need an editor for a textbook to be published next fall on insect anatomy. It's ---67.--- at upper-level university biology classes. I don't know if you are doing any editing work these days, but I remember you were a Biology major in college. The content is a little too tough for my regular editors and ---68.--- you might be interested. ---69.--- I'll pay ten percent over the usual rates if you can do it. Let me know. The sooner the better!

Mark

---

66. (A) blue   (B) sudden   (C) long time   (D) instant

67. (A) aimed   (B) applied   (C) designed   (D) edited

68. (A) I am certain   (B) I considered if
      (C) I wondered if   (D) I understand

69. (A) The book was edited in six weeks.
      (B) The deadline is in six weeks.
      (C) You have to decide in six weeks.
      (D) I have been thinking of asking you for six weeks.

117

Sunday Soda Wants Your Online Votes

Consumers will again have the unique opportunity to choose Sunday Soda Inc.'s next product. We are asking people to choose among three fantastic options by voting online ----70.---- Friday so production can start next week.

Due to past technical problems with our system, we have specially improved our website and security. We want to make sure each of our consumers leaves feeling confident that ----71.----.

After lost votes and multiple voting by others, this time we will require that consumers register online, typing in their name and e-mail address. There is also a 1-800-xxx-xxx number that people can call for support staff to walk them through the process.

----72.---- People will get to choose the products they consume before they are even produced!

The vote will also help Sunday Soda gather marketing research data and work out ----73.---- computer glitches with our new website.

Sunday Soda is the number two soft drink manufacturer in the world. They are also very involved in giving back to the local community through education scholarships and grants.

Be a part of the Sunday Soda community. Vote on www.SundaySoda.com!

---

70. (A) over   (B) between   (C) onto   (D) before

71. (A) count is their vote   (B) vote their counts
    (C) their vote counts   (D) vote counts their

72. (A) These guidelines will clean up process procedures.
    (B) This will be one of the most democratic processes in the market economy.
    (C) The voting will be officially launched this coming Friday.
    (D) The market economy is based on supply and demand.

73. (A) each   (B) much   (C) few   (D) any

Review Test 2

PART 7 [読解問題]

次の Notice を読んで、74.~75. の質問の答えとして最も適切なものをそれぞれ (A)～(D) より
選び、その記号を解答用紙にマークしなさい。

Cultural Tour

Monkville Board of Education will hold a fifteen kilometer walkathon tour of some of the area's outstanding cultural assets, June 23rd from 9:30 a.m. to 3:00 p.m., starting at All Saints Cathedral near Bexley Station on the Central Line and visiting the Nixon Memorial, the Dassault Open Air Museum, and the Melville cottage amongst other attractions. Participation is free and expert guidance is available in English, Spanish and Chinese.

Please click **here** to download the submission form. All forms must be sent to Monkville Boad of Education at cultural-assetdsk@mbe.org by July 17th.

For details, call 722-9320 on weekdays between 8:30 a.m. and noon, or between 1 p.m. and 5:15 p.m.

---

74. Which of the following would most likely NOT appear on the itinerary?

(A) An amusement arcade

(B) An archaeological site

(C) An opera house

(D) An art gallery

75. How long is the tour expected to take?

(A) Four hours

(B) Four and a half hours

(C) Five and a half hours

(D) Six and a half hours

次の article を読んで、76.～77. の質問の答えとして最も適切なものをそれぞれ (A)～(D) より選び、その記号を解答用紙にマークしなさい。

Introducing a High-Tech Warehouse in Green City

In a groundbreaking move, Green City has welcomed its first high-tech warehouse, revolutionizing the logistics landscape. This state-of-the-art facility, located in the heart of the city, integrates cutting-edge technologies such as artificial intelligence, robotics, and the Internet of Things (IoT) to streamline operations and enhance efficiency.

The warehouse boasts automated conveyor belts, robotic pickers, and advanced inventory management systems, ensuring swift and accurate order fulfillment. These innovations not only reduce human error but also significantly cut down processing time, allowing for 24/7 operations.

Local businesses are already reaping the benefits, with faster delivery times and improved stock management. The warehouse's eco-friendly design, featuring solar panels and energy-efficient systems, underscores its commitment to sustainability.

Residents and business owners alike are excited about the positive impact this high-tech hub will have on the local economy, marking a new era of technological advancement in Green City.

76. The word "streamline" in paragraph 1, Line 4, is closest in meaning to:
(A) complicate
(B) simplify
(C) execute
(D) expand

77. According to the article, what is one of the benefits of the high-tech warehouse in Green City?
(A) Stable room temperature control
(B) Slower delivery times
(C) Improved stock management
(D) Automatic baggage loading and unloading

Review Test 2

次の Text-message chain を読んで、78.～79. の質問の答えとして最も適切なものをそれぞれ (A) ～ (D) より選び、その記号を解答用紙にマークしなさい。

Alex Lee [10:55 A.M.]
Hey Jamie, did you get a chance to review the quarterly report?

Jamie Martin [10:57 A.M.]
Hi Alex, yes, I did. I think we need to add more details to the sales section. What do you think?

Alex Lee [10:59 A.M.]
I agree. Let's discuss it in the meeting later.

Jamie Martin [11:00 A.M.]
Sounds good. By the way, have you seen the new project proposal from Taylor?

Alex Lee [11:01 A.M.]
Yes, I have. It looks promising. We should definitely consider it for the next quarter.

Jamie Martin [11:02 A.M.]
Absolutely. I'll bring it up in the meeting as well.

Kevin Taylor [11:04 A.M.]
Hey team, just wanted to remind you about the client presentation tomorrow. Is everyone ready?

Alex Lee [11:05 A.M.]
Thanks for the reminder, Taylor. I'm just putting the final touches on my part.

Jamie Martin [11:06 A.M.]
Same here. We'll be ready to impress!

Kevin Taylor [11:07 A.M.]
Great! Let's make sure we're all on the same page. See you at the meeting.

78. What suggestions does Ms. Martin have regarding the quarterly report?

(A) To shorten the executive summary

(B) To add more details to the sales section

(C) To include more graphics

(D) To revise the financial projections

121

79. At 11:07 A.M., what does Kevin Taylor most likely mean when he writes, "... we're all on the same page"?

(A) He wants everyone to read the same document.

(B) He is asking if everyone has completed their tasks.

(C) He wants everyone to understand the plan for the client presentation.

(D) He is suggesting a team meeting to discuss the project proposal.

次の E-mail を読んで、80.～82. の質問の答えとして最も適切なものをそれぞれ (A)～(D) より選び、その記号を解答用紙にマークしなさい。

To:	Kevin Anderson <kanderson@crownmail.com>
From:	Margaret Martinez <mmartinez@jumbotours.com>
Date:	7 August
Subject:	Re: Tour Refund Request

Jumbo Tours
Bringing the World to You!

Dear Mr. Anderson,

--[1]--. I am sorry to hear about your health concerns on the morning of your scheduled Everglades Airboat Tour, on August 5th. I know the airboat ride can be bumpy at times and perhaps uncomfortable for those not feeling well. At Jumbo Tours, we always make customer care our highest priority. --[2]--.

However, our refund policy clearly states that tour cancelation requests must come no later than 24 hours in advance. --[3]-- According to that policy and because we did not receive your cancelation notice until after the tour was completed, we are unable to offer you a refund. --[4]--.

If you have any questions, please let me know. I also hope Jumbo Tours can be of service to you in future travel plans.

Sincerely

Margaret Martinez
Customer Services

Review Test 2

80. What prompted Anderson to delay cancelation of his tour?
(A) He did not know the ride would be bumpy.
(B) He only became ill that day.
(C) He felt the tour company was not prepared.
(D) He purchased a tour ticket 24 hours in advance.

81. What is the reason that Jumbo Tours did not refund the tour purchase?
(A) They make customer care a high priority.
(B) The tour lacked participants that day.
(C) The airboat ride is typically comfortable.
(D) The cancelation request was late.

82. In which of the positions marked [1], [2], [3], and [4] does the following sentences best belong?

"This is due to the preparations that the local tour company must make for the number of participants."
(A) [1]
(B) [2]
(C) [3]
(D [4]

123

次の Article を読んで、83.～85. の質問の答えとして最も適切なものをそれぞれ (A)～(D) より
選び、その記号を解答用紙にマークしなさい。

New Asian Restaurant
Brings Culinary Delight to Salt Rock

Salt Rock (October 20) – The culinary scene in Salt Rock just got a delightful upgrade with the grand opening of "Fuji Bistro", a new Asian restaurant that promises to tantalize taste buds with its fusion of traditional and modern flavors.

Located in the heart of Salt Rock, Fuji Bistro offers a diverse menu featuring dishes from various Asian cuisines, including Japanese, Chinese, Thai, and Korean. The restaurant's interior is a blend of contemporary design and traditional Asian elements, creating a warm and inviting atmosphere for diners.

Head Chef Hiroshi Tanaka, a renowned culinary expert, expressed his excitement about the opening. "We aim to provide an unforgettable dining experience by combining authentic flavors with innovative culinary techniques," he said.

Local residents have already started flocking to the restaurant, eager to try signature dishes like the spicy ramen, sushi rolls, and Korean BBQ. With its unique offerings and cozy ambiance, Fuji Bistro is set to become a favorite dining spot in Salt Rock.

83. According to the article, what is true about Fuji Bistro?
    (A) It will open on October 20.
    (B) It adds other Asian flavors to Japanese cuisine.
    (C) It offers a fusion of traditional and modern flavors.
    (D) It has a traditional Asian interior design.

84. What is indicated about the head chef of Fuji Bistro?
    (A) He is a newcomer to the culinary scene.
    (B) He prefers contemporary interiors.
    (C) He values both authentic flavors and innovative techniques.
    (D) He prefers a casual dining experience.

124

85. What is mentioned about residents in Salt Rock?

    (A) They are excited to try the new dishes at Fuji Bistro.

    (B) They want to meet the chef at Fuji Bistro.

    (C) They prefer traditional American cuisine.

    (D) They have not yet visited Fuji Bistro.

次の Advertisement と E-mail を読んで、86.~87. の質問の答えとして最も適切なものをそれぞれ (A) ~ (D) より選び、その記号を解答用紙にマークしなさい。

Part-time administrative assistant Wanted

BellStar Inc. is looking for an administrative assistant with excellent organizational and verbal skills. Bellstar is a high-tech equipment management company, which sells and leases high-tech equipment to IT businesses throughout the city. This is a part-time, contract position, and no previous experience is necessary. The job duties include:

* *

—**Answering the telephone and transferring calls**

—**Responding to e-mail messages**

—**Scheduling**

—**Ordering office supplies**

—**Data entry**

—**Maintaining and organizing records and files**

—**Supporting office staff as needed**

—**Coordinating staff meetings and seminars**

—**Preparing charts, graphs and tables for presentations**

* *

The candidate must have good computer skills and be proficient in major software applications. This position is Monday, Wednesday and Friday from 3:00 p.m. to 8:00 p.m. and is available immediately. The days and hours are flexible. College students are especially encouraged to apply. Interested candidates may send their resumes by e-mail to David Mensler at mensler@bellstarinc.com. Resumes are not returnable, and only short-listed candidates will be contacted for an interview.

125

To:	David Mensler <mensler@bellstar.com>
From:	Anisha Basheera < anishabasheera @jupitermail.net>
Date:	August 25
Subject:	The administrative assistant position

Dear Mr. Mensler,

My name is Anisha Basheera and I am a university student who is currently pursuing an MBA. I saw your want ad on an Internet job search site, and would like to apply for the position.

You will see on the resume attached that I have some experience as an administrative assistant for my father's company, Yamuna. Yamuna is a trading company. I spent two of my three-month summer vacations there doing many of the same duties that you have detailed in your ad. I enjoyed my work there very much and would like to try working for a different type of company. I am very interested in your business, and feel that I have a lot to offer to BellStar.

I hope you will give me the opportunity to have an interview with you. I look forward to hearing from you.

Sincerely yours,

Anisha Basheera

86. What does BellStar do?

(A) Offer IT services

(B) Trade goods

(C) Sell and lend machinery

(D) Repair high-tech equipment

87. What is one of the duties of the position?

(A) Make presentations

(B) Assist coworkers

(C) Lease equipment

(D) Attend seminars

Review Test 2

88. What can be inferred about the position?

(A) The working days and hours can be changed.

(B) It is only suitable for college students.

(C) Everyone who applies will be contacted.

(D) No previous computer experience is required.

89. How long did Ms. Basheera work for her father's company?

(A) Three months

(B) Six months

(C) One year

(D) Two years

90. Why does Ms. Basheera want to work for BellStar?

(A) She didn't like working for her father's company.

(B) She is very interested in working for IT businesses.

(C) She needs the working experience to complete her MBA.

(D) She wants to work for a company other than her father's.

次の Article と E-mail を読んで、91.~95. の質問の答えとして最も適切なものをそれぞれ (A) ~ (D) より選び、その記号を解答用紙にマークしなさい。。

Washington—Darnet Corp. announced today that it would name Gerald. R. Solomon its new CEO, replacing outgoing president Michael Garrison. Solomon was formerly the vice president of Jensen Industries, Darnet's chief competitor. Darnet held the highest percentage of market share in the semiconductor business until last year, when Jensen took over as the leader in the industry. Solomon has been credited for helping Jensen Industries take the number one spot. He quit the firm last May, however, citing "differences of opinion" with Jensen's CEO, Martin Weiss. A spokesperson for Weiss said today that the relationship between Weiss and Solomon remains amiable.

Garrison left Darnet amid speculation that his business practices have left Darnet struggling to stay on top in the industry. Garrison has been picked up by TechRise Corp., where he will serve as the new director, replacing retiring director Ronald Dawson.

Shares in Darnet rose 18 percent on the news, and analysts predict that its share prices will continue to rise. Shares in Jensen dropped by 14 cents per share. Analysts advise that investors should wait until they see its first quarter earnings before purchasing shares.

127

To:	ronalddawson@irismail.com
From:	Jeffery Howard <jefferyhoward@ irismail.com >
Date:	September 15
Subject:	Retirement

Dear Ron:

I just read a news article that mentioned your retirement, and wanted to send my best wishes and congratulations. I'm certain that you will be missed at TechRise, but you are sure to enjoy your retirement. I'm two years into mine, and I have never been happier. I finally have the time to play a few rounds of golf now and again.

I also read that our old friend Mike Garrison will be filling your shoes. I'm sure you had something to do with his appointment. Contrary to what was written about him in the article, I think he's a hard worker, and TechRise will definitely appreciate his expertise.

Once you've settled into your new life, why don't we play golf together? I would love to catch up and hear about how you've been the past few years. Give me a call in a couple of weeks and let me know when you'd like to get together.

Yours truly,
Howard

91. What is the main topic of the article?

(A) Ronald Dawson's retirement

(B) Jensen's drop in share price

(C) Gerald Solomon's appointment

(D) Jensen's market share percentage

92. Why did Solomon quit Jensen Industries?

(A) The CEO asked him to quit.

(B) He wanted to go into retirement.

(C) The company wouldn't make him CEO.

(D) He couldn't agree with his boss.

128

Review Test 2

93. What can be inferred about Darnet's share prices?

   (A) It will fall by 14 cents per share.

   (B) It will steadily rise.

   (C) It will rise by 18 percent next quarter.

   (D) It will drop significantly.

94. What is the main purpose of Howard's e-mail to Ronald Dawson?

   (A) To tell him how he is spending his retirement

   (B) To recommend Michael Garrison as his replacement

   (C) To offer to fill his shoes

   (D) To congratulate him on his retirement

95. How long has it been since Howard met Ronald?

   (A) Several years   (B) A few months

   (C) A couple of weeks   (D) A few days

次の 2 つの E-mail と 1 つの Advertisement を読んで、96.～100. の質問の答えとして最も適切なものをそれぞれ (A)～(D) より選び、その記号を解答用紙にマークしなさい。

From:	Al Jones <ajones@xcubemail.com>
To:	Jim Taylor <jtaylor@crownmail.com>
Date:	5 September
Subject:	Here's a great condo!

Hey, Jim! How are things?

I was wondering if you're still hunting for a new place. If so, I might have found you an option. I got this local real estate flyer in my mailbox yesterday and one of the spots looks terrific. I took a photo of the basic info. Please find it attached.

It's got two bedrooms, just like you want, plus a living room and dining room/kitchen. It was just remodeled too. It's on the sixth floor, but there's an elevator. The price is incredible – less than a hundred grand. It's a steal!

129

The location is not far from here, so I know the neighborhood -- lots of shopping and restaurants. The train into the city is about a ten-minute walk, but there is a bus stop right in front of the building.

Anyhow, give it a look. If interested, I'd inquire about it soon. It won't be on the market long.

Nothing much new with me. Had dinner with Griff last month and talked about college days until the wee hours. He says hi. Let's all get together for drinks some time.

Al

CONDOMINIUM FOR SALE

Location: Bridgeway Park
Building Name: Heatherton Heights
Layout: Two bedrooms, living room and dining room/kitchen
Floor: Sixth / Unit 602 (Elevator)
Size: 890 square feet
Balcony Size: 150 square feet
Direction facing: South
Construction date: 2012
Remodeled: 2023

Nearest Station: 10-minute walk – Bridgeway Park North on the City Central Line
Nearest Bus Stop: Heatherton Heights – in front of the building
No parking available
Price: $99,500 dollars
Monthly maintenance fee: $95 dollars

Review Test 2

From:	Jim Taylor <jtaylor@crownmail.com>
To:	Al Jones <ajones@xcubemail.com>
Date:	7 September
Subject:	Re: Here's a great condo!

Al,

Nice to hear from you and I wish you'd written about a month earlier!

I just bought a place in Madison. I am moving in next weekend, in fact. It's closer to my work than Bridgeway Park, but it is not nearly as big as what you sent me – or as new. On top of that, it was more expensive!

But I like it. It's on the ninth floor and the view is great. I can even see the mountains. The neighborhood is safe and quiet. The big thing is that it will cut my commuting time in half. That alone is worth the price. It comes with a parking place too.

Once I settle in, I'll invite you and the rest of the gang over for a housewarming party. It's been too long since we've got together!

Thanks for thinking of me and see you in maybe a month or so.

Jim

96. What seems to be the relationship between Jim and Al.

 (A) They are work colleagues.

 (B) They were members of a gang.

 (C) They went to college together.

 (D) They are real estate agents.

97. According to Jim's email, what would seem to be a negative factor in regards to the Heatherton Heights information that Al sent.

 (A) The Heatherton Heights condominium has no parking.

 (B) The Heatherton Heights condominium is costly.

 (C) The Heatherton Heights condominium has a balcony.

 (D) The Heatherton Heights condominium is a bit old.

98. What factor does Al seem to value the most in regards to the Heatherton Heights condominium?

(A) The shopping and restaurants

(B) The number of bedrooms

(C) The distance to the train.

(D) The price

99. Why does Al encourage Jim to look into the Heatherton Heights condominium soon?

(A) The price might increase.

(B) Griff is also interested.

(C) Someone else might buy it first.

(D) It has just been remodeled.

100. What has Al known about Jim's housing search?

(A) Jim hopes to see the mountains.

(B) Jim hopes for two bedrooms.

(C) Jim hopes for parking.

(D) Jim hopes for good shopping.

TOEIC® L&R
Review Test 1
解 答 用 紙

ID	No.								

フリガナ	
N A M E 氏　名	

LISTENING SECTION

PART 1

No.	ANSWER A B C D
1	Ⓐ Ⓑ Ⓒ Ⓓ
2	Ⓐ Ⓑ Ⓒ Ⓓ
3	Ⓐ Ⓑ Ⓒ Ⓓ

PART 2

No.	ANSWER A B C
4	Ⓐ Ⓑ Ⓒ
5	Ⓐ Ⓑ Ⓒ
6	Ⓐ Ⓑ Ⓒ
7	Ⓐ Ⓑ Ⓒ
8	Ⓐ Ⓑ Ⓒ
9	Ⓐ Ⓑ Ⓒ
10	Ⓐ Ⓑ Ⓒ
11	Ⓐ Ⓑ Ⓒ
12	Ⓐ Ⓑ Ⓒ
13	Ⓐ Ⓑ Ⓒ
14	Ⓐ Ⓑ Ⓒ
15	Ⓐ Ⓑ Ⓒ
16	Ⓐ Ⓑ Ⓒ
17	Ⓐ Ⓑ Ⓒ

PART 3

No.	ANSWER A B C D	No.	ANSWER A B C D
18	Ⓐ Ⓑ Ⓒ Ⓓ	33	Ⓐ Ⓑ Ⓒ Ⓓ
19	Ⓐ Ⓑ Ⓒ Ⓓ	34	Ⓐ Ⓑ Ⓒ Ⓓ
20	Ⓐ Ⓑ Ⓒ Ⓓ	35	Ⓐ Ⓑ Ⓒ Ⓓ
21	Ⓐ Ⓑ Ⓒ Ⓓ		
22	Ⓐ Ⓑ Ⓒ Ⓓ		
23	Ⓐ Ⓑ Ⓒ Ⓓ		
24	Ⓐ Ⓑ Ⓒ Ⓓ		
25	Ⓐ Ⓑ Ⓒ Ⓓ		
26	Ⓐ Ⓑ Ⓒ Ⓓ		
27	Ⓐ Ⓑ Ⓒ Ⓓ		
28	Ⓐ Ⓑ Ⓒ Ⓓ		
29	Ⓐ Ⓑ Ⓒ Ⓓ		
30	Ⓐ Ⓑ Ⓒ Ⓓ		
31	Ⓐ Ⓑ Ⓒ Ⓓ		
32	Ⓐ Ⓑ Ⓒ Ⓓ		

PART 4

No.	ANSWER A B C D
36	Ⓐ Ⓑ Ⓒ Ⓓ
37	Ⓐ Ⓑ Ⓒ Ⓓ
38	Ⓐ Ⓑ Ⓒ Ⓓ
39	Ⓐ Ⓑ Ⓒ Ⓓ
40	Ⓐ Ⓑ Ⓒ Ⓓ
41	Ⓐ Ⓑ Ⓒ Ⓓ
42	Ⓐ Ⓑ Ⓒ Ⓓ
43	Ⓐ Ⓑ Ⓒ Ⓓ
44	Ⓐ Ⓑ Ⓒ Ⓓ
45	Ⓐ Ⓑ Ⓒ Ⓓ
46	Ⓐ Ⓑ Ⓒ Ⓓ
47	Ⓐ Ⓑ Ⓒ Ⓓ
48	Ⓐ Ⓑ Ⓒ Ⓓ
49	Ⓐ Ⓑ Ⓒ Ⓓ
50	Ⓐ Ⓑ Ⓒ Ⓓ

READING SECTION

PART 5

No.	ANSWER A B C D
51	Ⓐ Ⓑ Ⓒ Ⓓ
52	Ⓐ Ⓑ Ⓒ Ⓓ
53	Ⓐ Ⓑ Ⓒ Ⓓ
54	Ⓐ Ⓑ Ⓒ Ⓓ
55	Ⓐ Ⓑ Ⓒ Ⓓ
56	Ⓐ Ⓑ Ⓒ Ⓓ
57	Ⓐ Ⓑ Ⓒ Ⓓ
58	Ⓐ Ⓑ Ⓒ Ⓓ
59	Ⓐ Ⓑ Ⓒ Ⓓ
60	Ⓐ Ⓑ Ⓒ Ⓓ
61	Ⓐ Ⓑ Ⓒ Ⓓ
62	Ⓐ Ⓑ Ⓒ Ⓓ
63	Ⓐ Ⓑ Ⓒ Ⓓ
64	Ⓐ Ⓑ Ⓒ Ⓓ
65	Ⓐ Ⓑ Ⓒ Ⓓ

PART 6

No.	ANSWER A B C D
66	Ⓐ Ⓑ Ⓒ Ⓓ
67	Ⓐ Ⓑ Ⓒ Ⓓ
68	Ⓐ Ⓑ Ⓒ Ⓓ
69	Ⓐ Ⓑ Ⓒ Ⓓ
70	Ⓐ Ⓑ Ⓒ Ⓓ
71	Ⓐ Ⓑ Ⓒ Ⓓ
72	Ⓐ Ⓑ Ⓒ Ⓓ
73	Ⓐ Ⓑ Ⓒ Ⓓ

PART 7

No.	ANSWER A B C D	No.	ANSWER A B C D
74	Ⓐ Ⓑ Ⓒ Ⓓ	89	Ⓐ Ⓑ Ⓒ Ⓓ
75	Ⓐ Ⓑ Ⓒ Ⓓ	90	Ⓐ Ⓑ Ⓒ Ⓓ
76	Ⓐ Ⓑ Ⓒ Ⓓ	91	Ⓐ Ⓑ Ⓒ Ⓓ
77	Ⓐ Ⓑ Ⓒ Ⓓ	92	Ⓐ Ⓑ Ⓒ Ⓓ
78	Ⓐ Ⓑ Ⓒ Ⓓ	93	Ⓐ Ⓑ Ⓒ Ⓓ
79	Ⓐ Ⓑ Ⓒ Ⓓ	94	Ⓐ Ⓑ Ⓒ Ⓓ
80	Ⓐ Ⓑ Ⓒ Ⓓ	95	Ⓐ Ⓑ Ⓒ Ⓓ
81	Ⓐ Ⓑ Ⓒ Ⓓ	96	Ⓐ Ⓑ Ⓒ Ⓓ
82	Ⓐ Ⓑ Ⓒ Ⓓ	97	Ⓐ Ⓑ Ⓒ Ⓓ
83	Ⓐ Ⓑ Ⓒ Ⓓ	98	Ⓐ Ⓑ Ⓒ Ⓓ
84	Ⓐ Ⓑ Ⓒ Ⓓ	99	Ⓐ Ⓑ Ⓒ Ⓓ
85	Ⓐ Ⓑ Ⓒ Ⓓ	100	Ⓐ Ⓑ Ⓒ Ⓓ
86	Ⓐ Ⓑ Ⓒ Ⓓ		
87	Ⓐ Ⓑ Ⓒ Ⓓ		
88	Ⓐ Ⓑ Ⓒ Ⓓ		

TOEIC® L&R
Review Test 2
解 答 用 紙

ID	No.							

フリガナ	
N A M E 氏 名	

LISTENING SECTION

PART 1

No.	ANSWER A B C D
1	Ⓐ Ⓑ Ⓒ Ⓓ
2	Ⓐ Ⓑ Ⓒ Ⓓ
3	Ⓐ Ⓑ Ⓒ Ⓓ

PART 2

No.	ANSWER A B C
4	Ⓐ Ⓑ Ⓒ
5	Ⓐ Ⓑ Ⓒ
6	Ⓐ Ⓑ Ⓒ
7	Ⓐ Ⓑ Ⓒ
8	Ⓐ Ⓑ Ⓒ
9	Ⓐ Ⓑ Ⓒ
10	Ⓐ Ⓑ Ⓒ
11	Ⓐ Ⓑ Ⓒ
12	Ⓐ Ⓑ Ⓒ
13	Ⓐ Ⓑ Ⓒ
14	Ⓐ Ⓑ Ⓒ
15	Ⓐ Ⓑ Ⓒ
16	Ⓐ Ⓑ Ⓒ
17	Ⓐ Ⓑ Ⓒ

PART 3

No.	ANSWER A B C D	No.	ANSWER A B C D
18	Ⓐ Ⓑ Ⓒ Ⓓ	33	Ⓐ Ⓑ Ⓒ Ⓓ
19	Ⓐ Ⓑ Ⓒ Ⓓ	34	Ⓐ Ⓑ Ⓒ Ⓓ
20	Ⓐ Ⓑ Ⓒ Ⓓ	35	Ⓐ Ⓑ Ⓒ Ⓓ
21	Ⓐ Ⓑ Ⓒ Ⓓ		
22	Ⓐ Ⓑ Ⓒ Ⓓ		
23	Ⓐ Ⓑ Ⓒ Ⓓ		
24	Ⓐ Ⓑ Ⓒ Ⓓ		
25	Ⓐ Ⓑ Ⓒ Ⓓ		
26	Ⓐ Ⓑ Ⓒ Ⓓ		
27	Ⓐ Ⓑ Ⓒ Ⓓ		
28	Ⓐ Ⓑ Ⓒ Ⓓ		
29	Ⓐ Ⓑ Ⓒ Ⓓ		
30	Ⓐ Ⓑ Ⓒ Ⓓ		
31	Ⓐ Ⓑ Ⓒ Ⓓ		
32	Ⓐ Ⓑ Ⓒ Ⓓ		

PART 4

No.	ANSWER A B C D
36	Ⓐ Ⓑ Ⓒ Ⓓ
37	Ⓐ Ⓑ Ⓒ Ⓓ
38	Ⓐ Ⓑ Ⓒ Ⓓ
39	Ⓐ Ⓑ Ⓒ Ⓓ
40	Ⓐ Ⓑ Ⓒ Ⓓ
41	Ⓐ Ⓑ Ⓒ Ⓓ
42	Ⓐ Ⓑ Ⓒ Ⓓ
43	Ⓐ Ⓑ Ⓒ Ⓓ
44	Ⓐ Ⓑ Ⓒ Ⓓ
45	Ⓐ Ⓑ Ⓒ Ⓓ
46	Ⓐ Ⓑ Ⓒ Ⓓ
47	Ⓐ Ⓑ Ⓒ Ⓓ
48	Ⓐ Ⓑ Ⓒ Ⓓ
49	Ⓐ Ⓑ Ⓒ Ⓓ
50	Ⓐ Ⓑ Ⓒ Ⓓ

READING SECTION

PART 5

No.	ANSWER A B C D
51	Ⓐ Ⓑ Ⓒ Ⓓ
52	Ⓐ Ⓑ Ⓒ Ⓓ
53	Ⓐ Ⓑ Ⓒ Ⓓ
54	Ⓐ Ⓑ Ⓒ Ⓓ
55	Ⓐ Ⓑ Ⓒ Ⓓ
56	Ⓐ Ⓑ Ⓒ Ⓓ
57	Ⓐ Ⓑ Ⓒ Ⓓ
58	Ⓐ Ⓑ Ⓒ Ⓓ
59	Ⓐ Ⓑ Ⓒ Ⓓ
60	Ⓐ Ⓑ Ⓒ Ⓓ
61	Ⓐ Ⓑ Ⓒ Ⓓ
62	Ⓐ Ⓑ Ⓒ Ⓓ
63	Ⓐ Ⓑ Ⓒ Ⓓ
64	Ⓐ Ⓑ Ⓒ Ⓓ
65	Ⓐ Ⓑ Ⓒ Ⓓ

PART 6

No.	ANSWER A B C D
66	Ⓐ Ⓑ Ⓒ Ⓓ
67	Ⓐ Ⓑ Ⓒ Ⓓ
68	Ⓐ Ⓑ Ⓒ Ⓓ
69	Ⓐ Ⓑ Ⓒ Ⓓ
70	Ⓐ Ⓑ Ⓒ Ⓓ
71	Ⓐ Ⓑ Ⓒ Ⓓ
72	Ⓐ Ⓑ Ⓒ Ⓓ
73	Ⓐ Ⓑ Ⓒ Ⓓ

PART 7

No.	ANSWER A B C D	No.	ANSWER A B C D
74	Ⓐ Ⓑ Ⓒ Ⓓ	89	Ⓐ Ⓑ Ⓒ Ⓓ
75	Ⓐ Ⓑ Ⓒ Ⓓ	90	Ⓐ Ⓑ Ⓒ Ⓓ
76	Ⓐ Ⓑ Ⓒ Ⓓ	91	Ⓐ Ⓑ Ⓒ Ⓓ
77	Ⓐ Ⓑ Ⓒ Ⓓ	92	Ⓐ Ⓑ Ⓒ Ⓓ
78	Ⓐ Ⓑ Ⓒ Ⓓ	93	Ⓐ Ⓑ Ⓒ Ⓓ
79	Ⓐ Ⓑ Ⓒ Ⓓ	94	Ⓐ Ⓑ Ⓒ Ⓓ
80	Ⓐ Ⓑ Ⓒ Ⓓ	95	Ⓐ Ⓑ Ⓒ Ⓓ
81	Ⓐ Ⓑ Ⓒ Ⓓ	96	Ⓐ Ⓑ Ⓒ Ⓓ
82	Ⓐ Ⓑ Ⓒ Ⓓ	97	Ⓐ Ⓑ Ⓒ Ⓓ
83	Ⓐ Ⓑ Ⓒ Ⓓ	98	Ⓐ Ⓑ Ⓒ Ⓓ
84	Ⓐ Ⓑ Ⓒ Ⓓ	99	Ⓐ Ⓑ Ⓒ Ⓓ
85	Ⓐ Ⓑ Ⓒ Ⓓ	100	Ⓐ Ⓑ Ⓒ Ⓓ
86	Ⓐ Ⓑ Ⓒ Ⓓ		
87	Ⓐ Ⓑ Ⓒ Ⓓ		
88	Ⓐ Ⓑ Ⓒ Ⓓ		

スコア550~600をめざす
TOEIC® L&R Test 実践チャレンジ

編著者	西 谷 恒 志	
	トム・ディロン	
	マイケル・シャワティ	
発行者	山 口 隆 史	

発 行 所　㈱音羽書房鶴見書店

〒113-0033　東京都文京区本郷 3-26-13
TEL 03-3814-0491
FAX 03-3814-9250
URL: https://www.otowatsurumi.com
e-mail: info@otowatsurumi.com

2025 年 3 月 1 日　初版発行

組版　ほんのしろ／装幀　吉成美佐(オセロ)
印刷・製本　(株) シナノ パブリッシング プレス
■ 落丁・乱丁本はお取り替えいたします。

EC-079